Golfing Gems

THE CONNOISSEURS GUIDE TO GOLF COURSES IN

SCOTLAND

First published in Great Britain 1997 by

BEACON BOOKS

Barn Oast, Woodfalls Industrial Estate, Laddingford, Maidstone, Kent ME18 6DA.

ISBN 1 901839 01 X

© Finley Brand Communications Ltd. 1997

The moral right of the publisher has been asserted.

Distributed by Macmillan Distribution Ltd. 01256 29242

Cover design by Roland Davies.

Course descriptions and photography by David Whyte.

Typesetting by Snap Graphics, Tunbridge Wells.

Repro by Chameleon Colour, Tonbridge.

Printed and bound in Italy.

This book may be ordered by post direct from the publisher, but please try your book shop first. Corporate editions and personal subscriptions of any of the Beacon Book guides are available. Call for details – tel: 01622 872400.

Also published in the series: **Golfing Gems of England & Wales**
                                  Golfing Gems of Ireland

Golf Monthly is published on the first Thursday of every month by IPC Magazines Limited, King's Reach Tower, Stamford Street, London SE1 9LS. For subscription enquiries call: 01444 445555 (fax no: 01444 445599) or write to: Quadrant Subscription Services, FREEPOST CY1061, Haywards Heath, West Sussex RH16 3ZA.

Contents

Acknowledgements

As with any new book there have been many people who have contributed enormously and without whose help the 'Gems' would have remained hidden. We thank them all but in particular wish to express our sincerest appreciation to the following: To Christine for keeping us organised, to Mike for his stylish subbing, to Nicola for keeping our spirits up and to Daisy for keeping us on our toes. But finally to you dear reader for deeming our effort worthy of your hard-earned cash. Many thanks.

Andrew Finley   *Robert Brand*

Foreword

Scotland – The Real Home of Golf

*E*ach season somewhere around 500,000 overseas visitors descend on Scotland to sample golf in the home of the game and that number is increased to well in excess of a million when one also takes into account visitors from England and elsewhere around the British Isles. Scotland remains one of the world's most popular golfing destinations and, while a small minority of the visitors still clamour for nothing more than a game on the Old Course, or one or two of the other venerable Open venues, more and more are starting to look further afield, too. At long last the most discerning visitors have discovered that there is a lot more to golf north of the border than the five courses which are currently on The Open rota.

Carnoustie, Muirfield, St. Andrews, Troon and Turnberry all have their undoubted charms, and will forever be the main attraction to the great mass of foreign visitors who grew up on a rich diet of the exploits of Henry Cotton, Peter Thomson, Arnold Palmer, Jack Nicklaus et al. But one should never lose sight of the fact that Scotland has a lot more to offer as well.

What the visitor must remember is that The Home of Golf has somewhere around 850 courses dotted about within its boundaries and most of those are well worth a game. A small number of the most exclusive facilities charge in excess of £75 for a round but most are still well under £30 a round and some charge a good deal less than that. Golf in Scotland still represents wonderful value for money which is why more and more visitors are travelling to the Home of Golf in their droves.

This book is dedicated to all those visitors who want to leave The Open trail behind and sample some of Scotland's other great golfing gems. It is hardly golf in the raw but it is golf as the Scottish play themselves and, as such, gives us a clear indication of what the game should be all about.

Within its pages we have featured 60 courses, from Dunbar and Hawick in the South to Brora and Fortrose & Rosemarkie in the north, and from Ladybank and Panmure in the east to Macrihanish and the wonderous Islay in the west. Our selection affords the visitor a huge variety of courses but one thing they have in common is that they all give the visitor a great golfing experience at an affordable price.

I hope you enjoy your golf.

Colin Callander

Regional Introduction Photographs:

Edinburgh & The South East - *The Glen*

Fife - *St. Andrews*

Tayside - *Glamis Castle*

Grampian - *Cruden Bay*

Highlands & Islands - *Durness*

Glasgow & South West - *Lamlash*

Back Cover - *Royal Dornoch*

Introduction

*W*elcome to *Golf Monthly Golfing Gems of Scotland,* the guide book written by golfers for golfers. Our aim has been to produce a series of guides for the touring golfer which will give not just the basic facts and geography of a course but will convey some sense of the atmosphere, the environment, the whole 'feel' that makes a great golf course what it is and often makes a less-than-famous course well worth a detour from the golfing equivalent of a motorway map.

Not that our 'Gems' are always hidden – it's just that some may be unfamiliar. But that is their attraction. One thing characterises them all – they have been chosen and described by *Golf Monthly* writers who have themselves enjoyed playing them. The clubs have not paid for their entries so what you have is a selection of courses guided only by the writers' belief that these are the courses the visitor will find rewarding and hospitable.

Here, then, are descriptions of 60 Scottish courses you will be delighted to play. They all offer an intriguing – sometimes robust – challenge to your golfing ability and, unfailingly, a warm welcome and glorious scenery.

Keep the guide in your car, it will become an essential companion when travelling on business or pleasure. The hotels featured have, in nearly all cases, been recommended by the relevant golf club and we feel sure that you will find them an excellent place to stay, be it for one night or a long weekend. Often the proprietors are keen golfers themselves ensuring good local knowledge and a steady supply of sympathy!

Other books in this series cover England & Wales and Ireland with more planned for the near future. Each year the listings will be reviewed to ensure that quality is maintained. To help us in this task, should you have any comments please contact us at *Golf Monthly,* we will be pleased to hear from you.

Happy golfing!

* Whether indicated or not in the guide it will always be advisable to book your tee-time in advance and establish questions of dress code etc. to avoid possible embarrassment.

International Dialling Codes

From Eire	0044	(delete first 0 of local number)
From USA	01144	(delete first 0 of local number)

Edinburgh & South East

Edinburgh & South East

*F*or a golf holiday, there are many advantages to choosing this part
of Scotland. Primarily, the nation's capital, Edinburgh, is a rich
cultural focal point that offers some of the best shopping, ample
accommodation, fine cuisine and night-life. But, surrounded by so many fine
golfing areas, Edinburgh's own golf amenities are often missed. More than
any Scottish city and perhaps more than any capital in Europe, Edinburgh
is one of the best-provided golf destinations. Royal Burgess and Bruntsfield
Links are two highly esteemed clubs on the west side of the city whilst the
well-known resort of Dalmahoy offers two fine courses. A little further out in
West Lothian. Murrayfield and the courses around Musselburgh are also great
venues to play. Most highly recommended is Edinburgh's flotilla of municipal
courses. Not only are they well-presented with all the traditions of Scottish
golf but the value-for-money is simply outstanding. Silverknowes is an
impressive public parkland course rolling down to the Firth of Forth with
wide fairways and wonderful greens, always in top form. On returning to
the clubhouse, golfers frequently comment about the great condition of the
course. Special mention must be given to the Braid Hills municipal courses.
Set to the south and overlooking the city's chimney pots as well as the
landmarks of Arthur's Seat and Edinburgh Castle, Braid No. 1 is one of
the finest heathland courses you will find, and that says nothing of its views.
Twenty miles east of Edinburgh's Princes Street is East Lothian. The courses
here need little introduction, Muirfield, Gullane No. 1, North Berwick's West
Links; courses to test the best golfers. But amongst them are numerous
shorter courses that offer the same terrain and challenge as these more well
known links. Accommodation in East Lothian is geared up to golfers, most
a short distance from the clubhouses. If you want to take advantage of
Edinburgh's nightlife or shopping, there is an excellent train service running
through most East Lothian towns that can have you in Princes' Street and

the heart of the city within half an hour. To the south and within an hour's drive of Edinburgh, is the Scottish Borders, an area not as well known for golf but, with a rapidly growing portfolio of courses, both of holiday and championship status, this is rapidly changing. The Par 72, 6,789-yard Roxburghe course near Kelso, has recently opened and is surely a venue for international tournaments of the near future. For the touring golfer, this entire region is a bounty. In close proximity to England, golfers from the south can reach it and be playing in a few short hours. Throughout Edinburgh and the south east, there are numerous venues, some not mentioned in this edition, such as East Lothian's Whitekirk or CastlePark, recently opened and very promising. In the Borders there are others such as Duns or Eyemouth that have extended to offer 18 holes and these too are much improved. To the west of this region, and still within a short drive of the nation's capital, are courses such as West Linton or Harburn in West Calder or Ratho Park on Edinburgh's western fringe. Each offers a uniquely different environment and a singular golfing challenge. For details of the Lothian and Edinburgh's Golf Pass ring 0131 558 1072 and the Scottish Borders 'Freedom of the Fairways Passport' telephone 018907 50678.

DUNBAR
GLEN
HARBURN
HAWICK
HIRSEL

LONGNIDDRY
MINTO
PEEBLES
ST BOSWELLS

Dunbar

*F*or any visitor who has explored this part of Scotland, the main course at Dunbar will be one they will return to.

Distanced by some 15 miles from East Lothian's golfing centre, generally considered to be Gullane, Dunbar is worthy of the excursion and should be included in any itinerary.

Once again, it is a course the average player can enjoy, with a marvellous, open aspect to many of the holes and room to manoeuvre within the fairways although you 'get what you hit', as the members say – the mark of any honest golf course.

After an easy Par 5, 1st, it is clear that the seaside holes, 4th to 17th, give the course its flavour. This is not to detract from the more parkland nature of the

opening and closing holes, well designed to take best advantage of a wide, natural amphitheatre.

One would not describe the seaside holes as links-like as they are quite flat. Being laid out, some hard by the beach with no protection at all from the wind, this is the real test of the course.

The 12th is a difficult Par 4 usually playing into the wind and requiring two very good shots to reach the green. The 16th is a remarkable Par 3 that, depending on the wind, can call for anything from a 9 iron to a 3 wood to cover its 166 yards.

Dunbar's greens are generously proportioned and receptive making it one of the most capacious, all-round courses in East Lothian and well worth a visit.

HOW TO GET THERE

Half mile east of Dunbar. 30 miles east of Edinburgh off the A1 on the A1087.

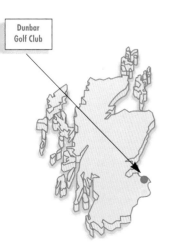

Dunbar
Golf Club

COURSE INFORMATION & FACILITIES

 Dunbar Golf Club
East Links, Dunbar
East Lothian EH42 1LT.

Secretary: Liz Thom.
Tel: 01368 862317. Fax: 01368 865202.

Golf Professional Tel: 01368 862086.

Green Fees:
Weekdays (Day) – £30. Weekends (Day) – £40.
Some time restrictions.

CARD OF THE COURSE – PAR 71

1	2	3	4	5	6	7	8	9	Out
477	494	172	349	148	350	386	369	507	3252
Par 5	Par 5	Par 3	Par 4	Par 3	Par 4	Par 4	Par 4	Par 5	Par 37

10	11	12	13	14	15	16	17	18	In
202	417	459	378	433	343	166	339	437	3174
Par 3	Par 4	Par 4	Par 4	Par 4	Par 4	Par 3	Par 4	Par 4	Par 34

13

Glen

*N*orth Berwick is one of East Lothian's best-loved holiday spots, its' two golf courses occupying either end of the town and both overlooking the sea.

The West Links is the better known and one of the finer examples of a links course but this should not preclude a visit to the Glen Golf Club on the eastern side of town.

It is a course full of character and this includes the elderly marshal who patrols the course on his ancient bicycle. Viewed from the 1st tee, the 1st and 18th holes are striking, both incorporating the climb up to the escarpment that this course is mainly laid out on. Once on the higher level, the views of the Bass Rock, the skerries (small islands), the Firth of Forth and back to the town itself, are quite remarkable.

The 5th is the course's most deceptive hole, a Par 4 of just over 300 yards with an island of rough impending to the right and a large, hidden declivity in front of the green. There is also OOB immediately behind in the form of a caravan site. Par here should be appreciated.

Looking back from the 8th tee you see the crumbling outline of Tantallon Castle but for a dramatic setting, there are few holes in Scottish golf to match the 13th , called the 'Sea Hole'. A Par 3 that can call for a pitching wedge one day and a 3-iron the next, it huddles amongst the beach and rocks.

One point to remember with the Glen as with most seaside courses, the greens, as a rule, lean towards the sea and you will rarely enjoy a straight putt

HOW TO GET THERE

1 miles east of town centre off A198 on the seafront – The course is signposted.

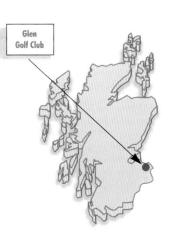

Glen Golf Club

COURSE INFORMATION & FACILITIES

The Glen Golf Club
East Links, Tantallon Terrace
North Berwick EH39 4LE

Secretary: Mr. D. R. Montgomery.
Tel: 01620 895288. Fax: 01620 895288.

Golf Professional Tel: 01620 894596.

Green Fees:
Weekdays – £16. Weekends – £20.
Weekdays (day) – £24. Weekends (day) – £28.

CARD OF THE COURSE – PAR 69

1	2	3	4	5	6	7	8	9	Out
333	373	349	184	369	476	381	357	207	3029
Par 4	Par 4	Par 4	Par 3	Par 4	Par 5	Par 4	Par 4	Par 3	Par 35

10	11	12	13	14	15	16	17	18	In
346	321	464	144	370	397	191	416	365	3014
Par 4	Par 4	Par 4	Par 3	Par 4	Par 4	Par 3	Par 4	Par 4	Par 34

Harburn

*I*f you are visiting Scotland's busy Central Belt and want to escape into the countryside, head for the village of West Calder, around 14 miles west of Edinburgh.

Harburn Golf Club, a couple of miles to the south of the village, is an ideal rural retreat yet only a short distance from the M8 motorway. It was at this location, the building of a great golf resort was considered. Instead the Caledonian Railway found, quite by chance, a spot further north in Perthshire and Gleneagles was created.

The Harburn clubhouse is most comfortable and with an admirable menu. The course is moorland verging on parkland with a good variety of beech, oak and pine trees.

Some may find it a bit short but it makes up for lack of length with some delightfully intricate tests. Many of the fairways slope either towards the gully and river or the railway line that passes along the course's southern flank.

The last four holes are perhaps the best, the 15th an excellent Par 3 onto a table-top green that is difficult to hold and can despatch a ball 50 feet down a ravine and into the burn.

The 16th plays over a deep gully while the 17th stretches out alongside the railway line and up to a tight green.

The final hole skirts round a hill and you are at an advantage if your left leg's shorter than your right.

COURSE INFORMATION & FACILITIES

Harburn Golf Club
Harburn, West Calder
West Lothian EH55 8RS

Secretary: John McLinden.
Tel: 01506 871131. Fax: 01506 871131.

Golf Professional Tel: 01506 871131.

Green Fees:
Weekdays – £16. Weekends – £21.
Weekdays (day) – £21. Weekends (day) – £32.

CARD OF THE COURSE – PAR 69

1	2	3	4	5	6	7	8	9	Out
326	385	142	480	214	334	426	383	516	3206
Par 4	Par 4	Par 3	Par 5	Par 3	Par 4	Par 4	Par 4	Par 5	Par 36

10	11	12	13	14	15	16	17	18	In
364	386	228	201	457	127	315	293	344	2715
Par 4	Par 4	Par 3	Par 3	Par 4	Par 3	Par 4	Par 4	Par 4	Par 33

HOW TO GET THERE

From Edinburgh: Take A71 to West Calder.
Golf Course is two miles south of West
Calder on B7008.

From Glasgow: Take M8 to Whitburn
Junction. Head for West Calder then
B7008 to Harburn.

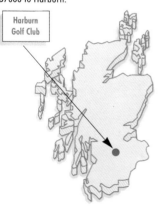

Harburn
Golf Club

Hawick

Hawick, pronounced locally as 'Hoik', is set on the banks of the Teviot River. Wool and its products have been Hawick's forte and famous names such as Pringle are the principal employers in town. You might, therefore, happen upon a photo-shoot on the 14th of Hawick's Vertish Hill course with Nick Faldo or Andrew Coultart posing in some new sweater.

But that is not the only reason famous appear at Hawick. In 1993, Faldo and Montgomerie played a round on this testing, upland venue and both had plenty to say in the positive. Nick Faldo was no stranger as he previously played with Tony Jacklin and shot a two under Par, 66.

Montie, on his visit, quipped that if there ever were a Himalayan Open, he would practice at Hawick. It 's not that bad but the opening two holes do climb and are fairly tight with the road and hillside rough on either side so there is no room for mistakes. This well-respected course then opens out to play over the top of Vertish Hill with no two holes the same. The 13th, 14th and 15th are the most beautiful with the 15th looking back down to town. The 18th is a rapidly descending Par 3, with the road out of bounds and a 'Postage Stamp' green.

Hawick along with all the Borders courses, is a member of the excellent *"Freedom of the Fairways"* Passport, a ticket that allows cheaper access to the participating courses. A 3-day passport costs £46.00 per person and the 5-day passport costs £70.00. For more details contact the Scottish Borders Tourist Board on Tel: 018907 50678

COURSE INFORMATION & FACILITIES

Hawick Golf Club
Vertish Hill
Hawick TD9 0NY.

Secretary: Mr. J. Harley.
Tel: 01450 374947.

Green Fees:
Weekdays – £18. Weekends – £18.
Weekdays (day) – £24. Weekends (day) – £24.
Weekend restrictions.

CARD OF THE COURSE – PAR 68

1	2	3	4	5	6	7	8	9	Out
195	350	388	325	338	445	449	144	430	3064
Par 3	Par 4	Par 4	Par 4	Par 4	Par 4	Par 4	Par 3	Par 4	Par 34

10	11	12	13	14	15	16	17	18	In
382	390	292	198	388	437	292	276	210	2865
Par 4	Par 4	Par 4	Par 3	Par 4	Par 4	Par 4	Par 4	Par 3	Par 34

HOW TO GET THERE

rom M6: A7 at Carlisle, head for
dinburgh, at first roundabout in town
mits turn sharp right. Head up hill,
ake left fork at top, continue to course.
rom Edinburgh: A7 through town
o roundabout (above). Just before
oundabout turn left then
p hill as above.

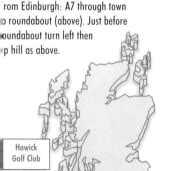

Hawick
Golf Club

Hirsel

The Hirsel Golf Club is in its third year as an 18-hole course and the new section is settling in very well. With a brand new clubhouse and some delightful challenges around this glorious parkland venue, this is another very welcomed member of the Scottish Borders, 'Freedom of the Fairways' programme.

The River Leet is a major, scenic feature of the course, crossing the fairways of some three holes but never presenting any real danger. The 1st dog-legs right down towards the river with high banking on either side of the corner. Mature stands of trees guard its flanks.

There is a confluence of holes at this point, rather confusing but soon untangled once you stand on the 2nd tee.

The 6th is a long Par 4 and although straightaway, it is the toughest on the front nine, often buffeted by a cross-wind although the trees to the right belie its impetus. The following 7th is a delightfully short Par 3 playing from on high across the river to a small green.

There are some stern tests on the more open reaches of the back nine. New trees have been planted and some older specimens exist. The 9th to the 12th play over this broad-backed rise, a good mix of lengths that call for most clubs in the bag.

The Hirsel estate that houses the course is just west of Coldstream and here you also find the Homestead Museum and Craft Centre, an old farmstead building offering a rare glimpse into the common tools and crafts formerly used in this area.

COURSE INFORMATION & FACILITIES

Hirsel Golf Club
Kelso Road, Coldstream
Berwickshire TD12 4NJ.

Secretary: John C. Balfour.
Tel: 01890-882233.
Fax: 01890-882233.

Green Fees:
Weekdays – £18. Weekends – £25.
Weekdays (day) – £18. Weekends (day) – £25.
Some time restrictions.

CARD OF THE COURSE – PAR 70

1	2	3	4	5	6	7	8	9	Out
304	290	246	320	372	357	170	345	420	2824
Par 4	Par 4	Par 3	Par 4	Par 4	Par 4	Par 3	Par 4	Par 4	Par 34

10	11	12	13	14	15	16	17	18	In
125	345	531	440	180	438	314	375	520	3268
Par 3	Par 4	Par 5	Par 4	Par 3	Par 4	Par 4	Par 4	Par 5	Par 36

HOW TO GET THERE

At west end of Coldstream
on the A697.

Hirsel
Golf Club

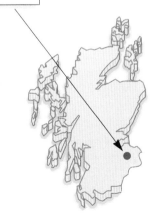

Longniddry

*O*n the south shores of the Firth of Forth, Longniddry is one of a host of courses that populate this area. It is chosen here because, in the midst of predominantly links courses such as Muirfield, Gullane Number 1 or North Berwick's West Links, Longniddry offers a slightly different character and one that many golfers enjoy.

Laid out by Harry Colt in 1921 over-looking Seton Sands, one would presume to play over the roll and pitch of a typical links layout but this is not the case.

The course presents itself in two distinct halves, the front being tighter and more enclosed with the second half being open and prey to the many winds that patrol this estuary. There are links characteristics to be found but established trees with many newer plantings coming into maturity soften this aspect making it more parkland. While variety is part of the appeal, it is the general quality of the course that makes is so popular, its fine properties endearing it to major tournaments but for its length at only 6,200 yards. Amongst the tougher holes is the 3rd, a long test on the Par 4 limit of 460 yards. There are no Par 5's at Longniddry, just long, defying Par 4's. For relief, the 6th is a gorgeous, short hole played from an elevated tee with trees surrounding the green.

The course has undergone a recent programme of development and the bunker hazards are now more formidable with newly turfed facing. Another area to avoid is the thick, rough grass, in some places standing at a foot high.

COURSE INFORMATION & FACILITIES

Longniddry Golf Course
Links Road, Longniddry
East Lothian EH32 0NL

Secretary/Manager: Neil Robertson.
Tel: 01875 852141. Fax: 01875 853371.

Golf Professional Tel: 01875 852228.

Green Fees:
Weekdays – £25. Weekends – £35.
Weekdays (day) – £38.
Handicap certificate required. Some time restrictions.

CARD OF THE COURSE – PAR 68

1	2	3	4	5	6	7	8	9	Out
398	416	461	199	314	168	430	367	374	3127
Par 4	Par 4	Par 4	Par 3	Par 4	Par 3	Par 4	Par 4	Par 4	Par 34

10	11	12	13	14	15	16	17	18	In
364	333	381	174	403	425	145	434	433	3092
Par 4	Par 4	Par 4	Par 3	Par 4	Par 4	Par 3	Par 4	Par 4	Par 34

HOW TO GET THERE

The course lies to the north of Longniddry Village, and is accessed via Links Road, in the village. Longniddry is approximately two miles north of the A1, and 17 miles east of Edinburgh City Centre.
Directions: From the A1, take the B6363 to Longniddry Village. Turn right and first left (down Links Road).

Longniddry Golf Club

GREEN CRAIGS

Green Craigs is located one mile west of Aberlady, on the coast road (A198) from Longniddry to North Berwick, "The White House on the Point"

We are a 'Restaurant first, Hotel second', given that we have six bedrooms, sleeping a maximum of 15 guests, but our Dining Rooms can seat 100 diners.
"Our reputation has been built around the quality of our food, wine and ambience!"
Tel: 01875 870301 or 306. Fax: 01875 870440.

Minto

*D*riving through the gates to Minto Golf Club, you immediately get an impression of what this course will be like. Sympathetically laid out through the aged groves of this beautiful estate, many of Minto's holes are graced with fine arboreal specimens.

Minto is an excellent parkland course tucked away behind the village of Denholm and overlooked by the imposing Rubers Law. It plays over ambling, gentle slopes for the first ten holes before opening out into wider plains at the 11th.

The 4th is a difficult Par 3 playing across the top of the course and on the level. Here, the course opens out and the main challenge is hitting the ball into the westerly wind. Despite being built on the side of a hill, there are no steep climbs although the view from the 12th tee, on a hole they call the Everest, can give rise to sudden palpitations. This is a short par 4 that suddenly ascends just before the pin.

At the moment, there are no bunkers on the course and the rough is fairly lenient but this is changing in order to present a greater challenge. Fairways are being narrowed and bunkers strategically placed. Much of this work will be completed by 1998 season. More trees are also being planted on the back nine.

Minto's clubhouse, is very modern, small but welcoming, and was built, to a large degree, by the club members.

COURSE INFORMATION & FACILITIES

Minto Golf Club
Minto
Hawick TD9 8SH

Secretary: Ian Todd.
Tel: 01450 870220 & 01835 862611.

Green Fees:
Weekdays – £15. Weekends – £20.
Weekdays (day) – £20. Weekends (day) – £25.
Some time restrictions.

CARD OF THE COURSE – PAR 68

1	2	3	4	5	6	7	8	9	Out
396	309	421	236	248	226	188	347	325	2696
Par 4	Par 4	Par 4	Par 3	Par 4	Par 3	Par 3	Par 4	Par 4	Par 33

10	11	12	13	14	15	16	17	18	In
252	369	267	311	409	355	297	122	375	2757
Par 4	Par 4	Par 4	Par 4	Par 4	Par 4	Par 4	Par 3	Par 4	Par 35

HOW TO GET THERE

North east of Hawick on A698 (5 miles).
Turn left at Denholm for Minto (1¼ miles), follow signs to golf course.

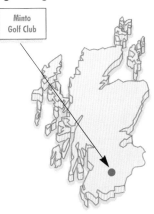

Minto Golf Club

Peebles

The Scottish Borders were often overlooked in the planning of past golf holidays. Now, with several magnificent 18 hole layouts including the new championship Roxburghe course and a clutch of 9 hole courses that are absolutely delightful to play on, this is no longer the case.

Peebles Golf Club must certainly be included on a Borders visit, renowned for its quality greens and outstanding views over this hospitable holiday town.

Standing on the 1st tee, overlooked by the impressive new clubhouse, it would be easy to decide that you are facing a mountain goat tract that will surely induce exhaustion by the 9th. Don't be alarmed! This is one of the most walkable courses in the Scottish Borders and the fine nature of the place soon takes precedence over any worries of weariness.

The first few holes do rise gradually but it is far from tasking and the distracting views over Peebles, the River Tweed and the surrounding hillsides, are reward enough. This Braid/Colt design actually benefits from the sloping terrain and the ledged greens and their sandy defences make a particular conclusion to several holes. Wind, another factor on this elevated and exposed course, blows down or across many fairways making the task of driving up a rise compounded and a seemingly well-struck shot often falls short. The 5th, presented in the top corner of the course, is a typical example and the two, steep-sided bunkers to the right can be particularly troublesome.

PEEBLES

HOW TO GET THERE

Peebles lies 23 miles south of Edinburgh in the Scottish Borders. The course is situated on north west side of the town.

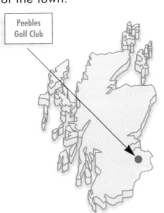

Peebles
Golf Club

COURSE INFORMATION & FACILITIES

Peebles Golf Club
Kirkland Street
Peebles EH45 8EU

Secretary: H. T. Gilmore.
Tel: 01721 720197.

Green Fees:
Weekdays – £18. Weekends – £24.
Weekdays (day) – £25. Weekends (day) – £34.
Some time restrictions.

CARD OF THE COURSE – PAR 70

1	2	3	4	5	6	7	8	9	Out
196	440	359	295	342	401	135	359	497	3024
Par 3	Par 4	Par 4	Par 4	Par 4	Par 4	Par 3	Par 4	Par 5	Par 35

10	11	12	13	14	15	16	17	18	In
365	326	173	319	377	431	193	411	541	3136
Par 4	Par 4	Par 3	Par 4	Par 4	Par 4	Par 3	Par 4	Par 5	Par 35

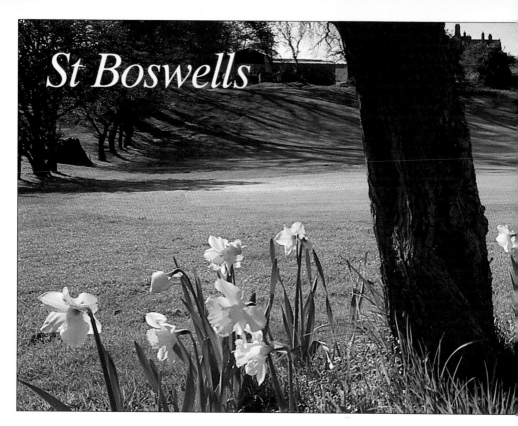

St Boswells

*T*he Scottish Borders, so long renowned for rivers, Rivers and rugby, is now rapidly establishing itself as a golfing focal point. With courses of world-class quality appearing and extensions to existing 9-hole layouts, there is now a range of golf that can equal most other parts of the country.

The existing 9-hole courses still offer excellent sport to holiday golfers and one of the best of these is St Boswells, a delightful design with eight of its nine holes set on the flat plain or 'haugh' of the River Tweed. The ruins of Dryburgh Abbey, burial ground of Sir Walter Scott, can just be seen above the trees on the opposite bank of the river and cuckoos and woodpeckers can be heard in the surrounding woods.

While some visitors will find some Borders courses too hilly, there is no such problem at St Boswells. Each hole on the course is simple in its character, most often flat with the occasional ancient tree overlooking the green, but greatly enhanced by such beautiful surrounding scenery. The 2nd tee gives a fine impression of the place, set high on a plateau, a Par 3 that drops to the small green. The River Tweed, defined as 'a lateral water hazard', comes into play on holes 4-6 – hook and you're in. Celebrating its centenary in 1999, St Boswells was laid out by Willie Park Jnr at the end of the last century. He thought the turf of St Boswells reminded him of a links course probably due to the alluvium soil built up by the river, which drains very quickly.

HOW TO GET THERE

The course is located in the centre of the Scottish Borders and is accessible only a short distance from Trunk route A68.

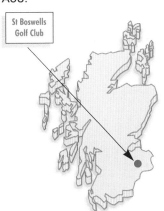

St Boswells
Golf Club

COURSE INFORMATION & FACILITIES

 St Boswells Golf Club
Braeheads, St Boswells
Nr Melrose TD6 0DE

Secretary: J. G. Phillips.
Tel: 01835-823527.

Green Fees:
Weekdays – £12. Weekends – £15.
Weekdays (day) – £15. Weekends (day) – £15.
Some time restrictions.

CARD OF THE COURSE – PAR 66

1	2	3	4	5	6	7	8	9	Out
148	161	316	198	425	321	430	370	256	2625
Par 3	Par 3	Par 4	Par 3	Par 4	Par 4	Par 4	Par 4	Par 4	Par 33

10	11	12	13	14	15	16	17	18	In
148	161	316	198	425	321	430	370	256	2625
Par 3	Par 3	Par 4	Par 3	Par 4	Par 4	Par 4	Par 4	Par 4	Par 33

Fife

Fife

There is little doubt that the Kingdom of Fife is the epicentre of the traditions of the game of golf. The streets of the 'Auld Grey Toon', St Andrews, reflect the ages through which the game has developed. Its ancient cathedral, towers and closes have witnessed the generations that have established and advanced the game. 600 years ago, 'gowf' was already a popular pastime for the town's inhabitants, playing for free over the wide links or 'common land' on the north edge of town. Today, its citizens still enjoy the advantage of cheap golf on the five, essentially municipal links courses that are still owned by the people of St Andrews. For the visitor too St Andrews represents good value, particularly if they take time to explore the courses less in demand than the famous Old. The Jubilee, the Eden and the New offer many of the flavours of the Old but each with its own traits. The Strathtyrum is the newer on the wide links and an easier proposition although, in a wind it can test the best. With the addition of the superlative Duke's course, two miles inland, St Andrews is a now the consummate golfing centre. With such a focus in the 'Auld Grey Toon', it is a wonder golfers ever discover the rest of Fife's golfing gems. But those that venture south along the coast, north and towards the Tay or inland to Ladybank or Dunfermline will unfold one of the richest golfing counties in Great Britain. Around the shores of the Firth of Forth to the East Neuk, are a string of golfing jewels. King James IV remarked that Fife was a "Kingdom fringed with gold" referring to the busy, trading sea-ports of the East Neuk. But today, it is a kingdom fringed with golf. The north of Fife is also plentiful with venues such as Scotscraig or the new Drumoig complex, home of the National Golf Centre. Shorter courses such as St Michael's have been encouraged to extend their number of holes to create equally inviting Tests. Most Fife towns have a golf course nearby, worthy of attention. Thornton has an excellent parkland, flat but very demanding if the wind blows. Balbirnie Park is laid out amidst a wooded estate while the courses in Kirkcaldy, both member's club and municipal, are most enjoyable. There are the Open qualifying courses such as at Lundin, Ladybank and Leven and the Pay and Play venues such as at Charleton. With so much variety and number it would be difficult to cover the majority of Fife's courses even in several visits. For non-golfing excursions, apart from St Andrews' obvious attractions, the East Neuk villages are highly recommended. If children are looking for a day out, Deep Sea World in North Queensferry is an award winning underwater adventure while Dunfermline, and villages such as Falkland and Culross offer a rich taste of the Kingdom's history.

ABERDOUR
CRAIL
DRUMOIG
LADYBANK

SCOTSCRAIG
ST ANDREWS – DUKES
ST ANDREWS – JUBILEE

Aberdour

*F*ive miles east of the Forth Bridges, the village of Aberdour commences a series of delightful seaside hamlets that skirt the Firth of Forth.

Aberdour's golf course is a parkland that runs along the shore with views of historic Inchcolm Abbey set on a string of rocky islands as well as the city-scapes of Edinburgh on the opposite side of the river.

With some illustrious neighbours just a few miles to the north Aberdour stands the chance of being missed but once it has been sampled, most golfers highly recommend it.

It is with an inspiring backdrop that this compact little course starts.

The 1st plays directly towards the Abbey from a high tee with the beach and a dyke to the left. It is a tricky opener especially in a wind and if you have not played the course before. This type of pressure persists through holes 2 and 3 with the 2nd being a delectable Par 3 played over the bay.

The flavour is far more parkland as you turn uphill to the 5th. Then there is a set of newer holes, 7th to 9th with the 8th, a Par 4 of 458 yards being the biggest challenge on the course. OOB stretches down the left with a ditch cutting across the middle of the fairway about 135 yards from middle of the green. But it is the approach that is most difficult with a hazardous mound to the right.

FIFE

HOW TO GET THERE

M90 junction 1 just north of Forth Bridge. Take A921 (east). Three miles to Aberdour. At Forresters Arms, in middle of village, turn south down Shore Road then third left into Seaside Place.

Aberdour
Golf Club

COURSE INFORMATION & FACILITIES

Aberdour Golf Club
Seaside Place
Aberdour, Fife KY3 0TX

Secretary: J. J. Train.
Tel: 01383 860080. Fax: 01383 860050.

Golf Professional Tel: 01383 860256.

Green Fees:
Weekdays – £17. Weekdays (day) – £28.
Some time restrictions.

CARD OF THE COURSE – PAR 67

1	2	3	4	5	6	7	8	9	Out
159	159	343	287	359	365	163	458	394	2687
Par 3	Par 3	Par 4	Par 4	Par 4	Par 4	Par 3	Par 4	Par 4	Par 33

10	11	12	13	14	15	16	17	18	In
530	340	163	251	315	171	449	354	197	2773
Par 5	Par 4	Par 3	Par 4	Par 4	Par 3	Par 4	Par 4	Par 3	Par 34

35

Crail

C rail Golfing Society plays over Balcomie Links, a couple of miles north of the East Neuk village of Crail and around 12 miles southwest of St Andrews

The clubhouse, set on the tip of Fife Ness, looks down upon the closing four holes and the North Sea. First impression of the course is that there is room for error but don't depend on it especially if there is any wind and there usually is. The 1st plays down to sea level from a high tee with a lifeboat shed standing right of the green. This vantage point should give you a fair impression of the strength of the day's wind.

If you haven't taken account of the wind on the 1st, the 2nd will sharpen your wits when the ball is pushed 'out of bounds' on to the beach. Whichever way the wind blows, usually from the west, it is a strongly determining factor on most of Crail's holes.

The newly designed Par 4, 5th (Hell's Hole) is amongst the most challenging in Scotland, a magnificent right dog-leg playing over the craggy rocks of a bay. No matter what the conditions, it pays to lay up safely here, resisting the urge to fly towards the pin, inviting though it might be.

The 13th is a 200-yard, Par 3 up a high defensive embankment. This is immediately followed by a delightful 14th, Par 3 back down to sea level again. Look out for seals basking on the rocks along this stretch and there are often gannets out at sea diving for fish.

COURSE INFORMATION & FACILITIES

Crail Golfing Society
Balcomie Clubhouse, Fifeness
Crail, Fife KY10 3XN.

Manager: J. F. Horsfield.
Tel: 01333 450686. Fax: 01333 450416.

Golf Professional Tel: 01333 450950.

Green Fees:
Weekdays – £19. Weekends – £24.
Weekdays (day) – £30. Weekends (day) – £38.
Some time restrictions.

CARD OF THE COURSE – PAR 69

1	2	3	4	5	6	7	8	9	Out
328	494	184	346	459	186	349	442	306	3094
Par 4	Par 5	Par 3	Par 4	Par 4	Par 3	Par 4	Par 4	Par 4	Par 35

10	11	12	13	14	15	16	17	18	In
336	496	528	219	150	270	163	463	203	2828
Par 4	Par 5	Par 5	Par 3	Par 3	Par 4	Par 3	Par 4	Par 3	Par 34

HOW TO GET THERE

From Edinburgh follow A92 to Kirkaldy, then the A915 to Leven. Take B942 to Pittenweem. Follow the A917 to Crail. From Dundee take A91 onto St Andrews, then the A917 to Crail

Crail
Golf Club

Drumoig

Drumoig Golf Club and Hotel is a new course and golfing complex that has opened only 8 miles north of St Andrews.

As the base for the newly-formed Scottish National Golf Centre and Scottish Golf Union, the course is obliged to be of the highest championship standard.

Already it is gaining such acclaim. Of necessity, it is long – 7,000 yards off the back tees but even from the forward boxes it plays all its length and requires conscientious application of the big clubs.

A 25-foot quarry accentuates the course's signature holes. The 5th is a Par 5, usually into the prevailing wind, which often requires two woods and a 5 iron. It is a strenuous test, created mainly by nature except for the pot bunker placed just in front of the green.

On the other side of the quarry, the 13th creates another dilemma where a drive and wedge can get you to the green but this is a much smaller target and it is here you can come unstuck.

The 9th and 10th have created an American effect where water threatens off the tees but it also offers a stirring view of the Fife countryside. There is little doubt that Drumoig will become one of Scotland's premier venues, much as Loch Lomond has, so play it soon. At present, it is easy to get tee times, even at weekends and green fees are most reasonable.

COURSE INFORMATION & FACILITIES

Drumoig Golf Club
Drumoig, Leuchars
St. Andrews, Fife KY16 0BE.

Director of Golf: Jim Farmer.
Tel: 01382 541800. Fax: 01382 542211.

Golf Professional Tel: 01382 541800.

Green Fees:
Weekdays – £20. Weekends – £24.
Weekdays (Day) – £35. Weekends (Day) – £43.
Society Rates: Reduced rates for groups.

CARD OF THE COURSE - PAR 72

1	2	3	4	5	6	7	8	9	Out
432	218	563	214	565	430	379	358	434	3593
Par 4	Par 3	Par 5	Par 3	Par 5	Par 4	Par 4	Par 4	Par 4	Par 36
10	11	12	13	14	15	16	17	18	In
396	340	422	300	202	582	190	539	442	3413
Par 4	Par 4	Par 4	Par 4	Par 3	Par 5	Par 3	Par 5	Par 4	Par 36

HOW TO GET THERE

Drumoig is on the A92, St. Andrews, Dundee Road, 9 miles from St. Andrews. From Glasgow or Edinburgh drive north on M90 from Forth Bridge and take St. Andrews turn off. Turn left onto A92 at Guardbridge and follow Dundee signs. Drumoig is 4 miles before Dundee.

Drumoig Golf Club

THE SANDFORD

COUNTRY HOUSE HOTEL
Newton Hill
Wormit
Nr. Dundee
FIFE DD6 8RG
SCOTLAND

Telephnone:
01382 541802
Fax:
01382 542135

The Sandford Country House Hotel
A few minutes from Dundee and St. Andrews, is owned and run by the Cowan family. Built at the turn of the century and set in seven acres, it offers comfortable en-suite accommodation in the most tranquil of surroundings. The Sandford offers excellent Scottish and European cuisine – accompanied by fine wines.

Ladybank

Set at the heart of Fife's Kingdom, Ladybank Golf Club plays over heathland avenues delineated by Scots Pine, Silver Birch and shrouds of heather.

Its standard is exceptional, used as an Open Qualifier but usually it is a quiet and peaceful place where you can play without distraction. Set in a natural amphitheatre surrounded by the Howe of Fife with the Lomond Hills to the southwest, red squirrels, now quite rare in the area, live in the trees.

Old Tom Morris designed the first six holes before it was extended to a full layout. Being inland and well protected by the flanks of firs, wind is not so much of a factor. If you stray into the trees and heather you are punished but staying straight and not trying to cut corners can profit.

The 2nd gets the game underway, a long Par 5 of 548 yards calling for full strikes all the way. The 9th is a 401-yard dog-leg. At around 180 yards off the tee, there stands a huge Scots Pine, which will interfere with ambitious drives. Take an iron off the tee for position and deal with a long second shot to the green. Oh, by the way, there is a large dip in front of the green, which must be carried.

On the back nine, the 14th stands out, 413 yards off the back tees and usually into the prevailing wind with 200 yards to cover just to get on to the fairway.

COURSE INFORMATION & FACILITIES

Ladybank Golf Club
Annsmuir, Ladybank
Cupar, Fife KY15 7RA.

Secretary: I. F. Sproule.
Tel: 01337 830814. Fax: 01337 831505.

Golf Professional:
Tel: 01337 830725.

Green Fees:
Weekdays – £28. Weekends – £35.
Weekdays (day) – £38. Weekends (day) – £35.

CARD OF THE COURSE – PAR 71

1	2	3	4	5	6	7	8	9	Out
374	548	391	166	344	372	543	159	401	3298
Par 4	Par 5	Par 4	Par 3	Par 4	Par 4	Par 5	Par 3	Par 4	Par 36

10	11	12	13	14	15	16	17	18	In
165	407	243	528	413	390	398	387	408	3343
Par 3	Par 4	Par 3	Par 5	Par 4	Par 4	Par 4	Par 4	Par 4	Par 35

HOW TO GET THERE

Ladybank Golf Club is situated north of Glenrothes on the A914

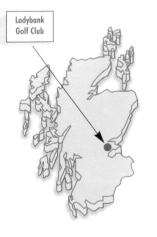

Ladybank
Golf Club

41

Scotscraig

Scotscraig Golf Club is situated just ten miles north of St Andrews in the charming North Fife village of Tayport. Established in 1817, when there were only twelve other golf clubs in existence, Scotscraig emanates a sense of tradition and hospitality to its many visitors. The present course was laid out by James Braid in the 1920's and is an Open Qualifying venue when the Open is held at St Andrews.

This is one of those enigmatic courses, not a true links nor heathland, nor even park but an interesting combination of all. Its fairways, especially on the front nine, billow with the knobbly characteristics of land that was once washed with rolling sea waves. From the 1st, you will find fairways that are not over-generous but accommodating enough to the simple, straight strike. Many find it preferable to use irons off the tees throughout the front half.

The 4th hole, a Par 4 of 365 yards, presents the course at its most challenging with a strategic decision whether to drive to get close to the green or lay up safely, but then face a long lob to a very difficult target.

The back nine is more in tune with an inland course. A new green at the 14th has made it a genuine three-shotter at over 500 yards. Generally speaking, Scotscraig is a test of accuracy rather than length and will reward the player who studies the form and plans each stroke with the next in mind. Catering in the clubhouses's Playfair Room or Maitland-Dougall Lounge is of a particularly high standard.

COURSE INFORMATION & FACILITIES

Scotscraig Golf Club
Golf Road, Tayport, Fife,
Scotland DD6 9DZ.

Secretary: K. Gourlay.
Tel: 01382 552515. Fax: 01382 553130.

Golf Professional
Tel: 01382 552855. Fax: 01382 553130.

Green Fees:
Weekdays – £27.00. Weekends: £32.00.
Weekdays (day) – £36.00.

CARD OF THE COURSE – PAR 71

1	2	3	4	5	6	7	8	9	Out
402	374	214	366	402	150	401	387	484	3180
Par 4	Par 4	Par 3	Par 4	Par 4	Par 3	Par 4	Par 4	Par 5	Par 35

10	11	12	13	14	15	16	17	18	In
404	459	389	165	523	175	479	380	396	3370
Par 4	Par 4	Par 4	Par 3	Par 5	Par 3	Par 5	Par 4	Par 4	Par 36

HOW TO GET THERE

) miles north of St Andrews. Follow the A919 &
)45 to Tayport or 4 miles south-east of Dundee
ver the Tay Road Bridge. Following the B945
ast to Tayport. From Tayport,
ne route to the club is well
gnposted. Nearest airports:
undee (5 miles), Edinburgh
0 miles), nearest train
ation: Leuchars
5 miles.

Scotscraig
Golf Club

The Duke's

The Duke's course is a relatively new layout overlooking St Andrews. It is classed as a blend of inland and links; the front nine weaves through woodland with flat greens while the back offers links-like rolling fairways and undulating greens.

One of the best challenges on the front nine is the 2nd which curves through woods, a slight dog-leg right best played up the left to gain sight of the green.

The 8th called 'Fair Dunt' is a Par 3, 212 yards usually into the westerly prevailing wind with a large pot bunker at front centre so its as important to err on the long side rather than short.

The back nine has spectacular views over St Andrews, the golf courses and sea.

To the north the Grampian Mountains come into prospect especially from the 13th aptly entitled, 'Braw View'.

The 14th, a 472 yard, Par 4, is where designer Peter Thomson discovered a natural spring and decided to incorporate it into the hole. It emanates at a stone mound around 200 yards off the tee then streams to the right. The best approach here is to drive right giving the shortest distance to the pin but beware of water and the large beech tree that can block out the green.

The 18th is the exceptional finish to this fine course. It rises gradually from tee to green with a large oak tree on the right at 280 yards. The two tiered green can be tricky so add an extra club length to be sure of safely reaching it.

COURSE INFORMATION & FACILITIES

The Duke's Golf Course
St. Andrews
Fife KY16 9SP

Secretary: Stephen Toon.
Tel: 01334 479947
Fax: 01334 479456

Green Fees:
Summer – £50.
Winter – £25.

CARD OF THE COURSE – PAR 72

1	2	3	4	5	6	7	8	9	Out
517	448	156	439	375	565	467	212	415	3594
Par 5	Par 4	Par 3	Par 4	Par 4	Par 5	Par 4	Par 3	Par 4	Par 36

10	11	12	13	14	15	16	17	18	In
429	610	212	397	472	533	429	191	404	3677
Par 4	Par 5	Par 3	Par 4	Par 4	Par 5	Par 4	Par 3	Par 4	Par 36

HOW TO GET THERE

⬛ towards St Andrews. At Guardbridge
⬛ge (approx 3¹/₂ miles) continue through
⬛ge and take right turn signposted
⬛thkinness. Head for Strathkinness
⬛ge and after passing through go
⬛r junction towards Craigtoun. At next
⬛ction turn left following sign
⬛raigtoun. The Dukes is
⬛ut half mile
⬛ the right.

**The Dukes
Golf Club**

OLD COURSE HOTEL
ST ANDREWS
GOLF RESORT & SPA

*Located in the heart of the home of golf, the hotel is stunningly situated overlooking the
infamous 17th Road Hole and the historic Royal and Ancient Clubhouse.*

*Just step through the entrance to discover why the Old Course Hotel has been described
as one of Europe's leading resort hotels.*

*Residents will also enjoy privileges at the Duke's Course including a reduction in green
fees and the opportunity to reserve tee-times when booking hotel accommodation.*

For further information contact:
RESORT RESERVATIONS, OLD COURSE HOTEL, ST ANDREWS, KINGDOM OF FIFE KY16 9SP
TELEPHONE: (01334) 474371 FAX: (01334) 477668

St. Andrews
(Jubilee)

For the golfing visitor to St Andrews who may not wish to endure the ballot or expense of the Old Course there are plenty of sound alternatives.

The Strathtyrum is the easiest of the 18-hole layouts, the Eden a moderate test and the New, quite demanding with, some would say, as much character than the Old without the quirkiness.

The Jubilee course, now in its 100th year and named to coincide with Queen Victoria's Diamond Jubilee, was originally only 12 holes long and then regarded as 'the Ladies course'. It was later lengthened and in recent years has undergone some major structural changes. It was not without its critics and quite rightly so but, with some excellent adaptions by Donald Steel, the Jubilee is now emerging as an excellent test. Its centenary means that many golfers are discovering it for the fine challenge that it now is. There are two overall factors to the course, its length and its open aspect to the West Sands and North Sea.

Lying on the southern flank of the peninsula that contains all the St Andrews links courses, the Jubilee catches the full effect of wind and weather. Adding this to its 6,800 yards, many are surprised how rigorous a course it can be.

It opens with a poor Par 4 but at the 2nd the new flavour of the course begins with a sprightly dog-leg to a tiered and well-protected green. There are many more such lively holes ahead and, coupled with its prodigious span, most golfers come off the Jubilee well tested.

COURSE INFORMATION & FACILITIES

St. Andrews Links
Fife
KY16 9SF.

Secretary:
D. N. H. James.
Tel: 01334 466666.
Fax: 01334 466664.

Green Fees:
Weekdays – £25/20 (high/low season).

CARD OF THE COURSE (Jubilee) – PAR 72

1	2	3	4	5	6	7	8	9	Out
454	336	546	371	162	498	373	369	192	3301
Par 4	Par 4	Par 5	Par 4	Par 3	Par 5	Par 4	Par 4	Par 3	Par 36
10	11	12	13	14	15	16	17	18	In
411	497	538	188	438	356	428	211	437	3504
Par 4	Par 5	Par 5	Par 3	Par 4	Par 4	Par 4	Par 3	Par 4	Par 36

HOW TO GET THERE

From Edinburgh and the south: Travel north on the M90 over the Forth Bridge. Leave the Motorway at Junction 3 and follow the A92 to its junction with the A914 north of Glenrothes. Take the A914 to the next roundabout, turn right and continue on the A91 through Cupar to St Andrews. From Perth and the north: Travel south on the M90 and exit at Junction 7. Drive through Milnathort and continue on the A91 through Auchtermuchty and Cupar to St. Andrews.

St. Andrews Golf Club

Tayside

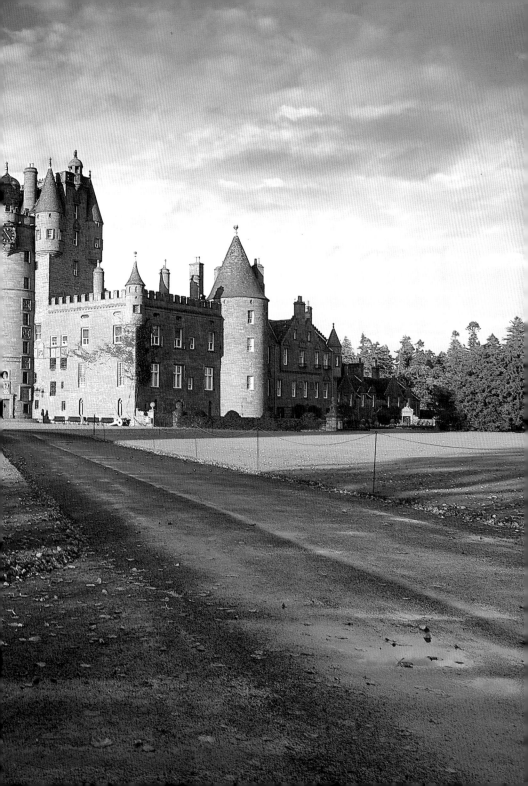

Tayside

*T*ayside is one most diverse areas of Scotland. From the East Coast bordering the North Sea to the highland heartland, it covers the important counties of Perthshire and Angus. Dundee is its largest city while Perth, Montrose and Kinross are busy centres. With the Highland Boundary Fault running southwest through both Angus and Perthshire, there is a backdrop of beautiful, heather-clad hills to the courses, while in Perthshire itself, many of the courses nestle in secluded upland glens. The Gleneagles complex is an elegant example of moorland put to its best use. With three spectacular 18 hole courses, a nine hole, 'Wee Course' and an excellent teaching and practice area, there is plenty of golf here although, it is strictly for guests of the Gleneagles Hotel. The newest Monarch course is more American in character but the two older courses are delightful James Braid layouts. Blairgowrie is also a magnet for golfers with the Rosemount course being the best known; however, the neighbouring Lansdowne course is very testing especially off the tees. For a more economic golfing break, there are few better deals than the Perthshire Highland Golf Ticket where you can play a day's golf on any of five participating 9-hole courses. If you choose to stay in one area such as Dunkeld, you can spend all your 5-day ticket on that course or you can travel to any of the others – the choice is yours. There is also the good-value Perthshire Green Card allowing five rounds on participating 18-hole courses. The Vale of Strathmore has become, in recent years, a compact parcel of excellent golf courses and a good base from which to stay and play any of these splendid layouts. From Blairgowrie through Alyth to Kirriemuir and Forfar, it would be possible to spend a week here sampling each of these excellent venues and, in non-golfing time, visit famous Glamis Castle, birthplace and ancestral home of HRH the Queen Mother or head into the peaceful Angus Glens The coast offers some of Tayside's best stretches of golf with Carnoustie at the heart of a dozen links layouts fringing the North Sea coast. Nearby are the Panmure or Monifieth courses, offering the highest standards and traditions of the game. Further north are the links courses of Montrose; the Medal being the superior, a course not unlike the reputable dune-shadowed links of the Aberdeen area. The city of Dundee, a good base for touring both Fife and Tayside, has three of its own courses with Downfield on the city's northern boundary, the best known. Two good municipal layouts are found at Caird Park and Camperdown Park. For diversion, the cities of Dundee or Perth offer good shopping centres with Crieff, Montrose or Blairgowrie presenting speciality outlets with the best of Scottish woollens and many other gift ideas of a uniquely Scottish flavour. For details on the Perthshire Highland Golf Ticket and the Perthshire Green Card contact Perthshire Tourist Board's Activity Line on 01738444144. For details of golf in Angus & the City of Dundee telephone 01369 708004.

ALYTH

BLAIRGOWRIE

CARNOUSTIE

CRIEFF

DOWNFIELD

DUNKELD & BIRNAN

EDZELL

FORFAR

KILLIN

KIRRIEMUIR

PANMURE

TAYMOUTH CASTLE

Alyth

The verdant Vale of Strathmore stretches through Perthshire and Angus, east towards Montrose on the coast and has become a hidden valley of golf where there are now a dozen delightful courses all within easy driving distance.

At its centre is Alyth Golf Club, a well-conceived heathland layout established over 100 years ago, the original 9 holes by Old Tom Morris, later extended and refined by James Braid. The combination of tree-lined fairways and diverse, rolling terrain makes this a superior test with a configuration that demands constant attention

Therefore, the emphasis is on precision rather than distance although both are needed at the course's most demanding stretch, the 9th, 10th & 11th, two long par 4's followed by a par 5. With a tight tee shot in every instance, this is the area to make or break a card.

On the front nine, the 5th is the hole everyone remembers with two stretches of burn intersecting the dog-legged fairway. The temptation is to fly towards the green and carry both burns but the canny club golfer, having been in the burn or OOB many times, prefers to go for the island and lob a safe 8 or 9-iron onto the tabletop green.

Alyth's most demanding aspect, however, might be its tranquil setting. Within the pines, sliver birch and heather and overlooking the nearby hills, it is easy to lose yourself in the joys of a good game of golf with a layout so conceived that you barely notice other groups of golfers.

COURSE INFORMATION & FACILITIES

Alyth Golf Club
Pitcrocknie
Alyth PH11 8HT.

Managing Director: J. Docherty.
Tel: 01828 632268. Fax: 01828 633491.

Golf Professional Tel: 01828 632411.

Green Fees:
Weekdays – £18. Weekends – £23.
Weekdays (day) – £27. Weekends (day) – £32.

CARD OF THE COURSE – PAR 70

1	2	3	4	5	6	7	8	9	Out
398	417	155	368	325	388	130	255	456	2892
Par 4	Par 4	Par 3	Par 4	Par 4	Par 4	Par 3	Par 4	Par 4	Par 34

10	11	12	13	14	15	16	17	18	In
436	504	308	318	198	446	545	202	356	3313
Par 4	Par 5	Par 54	Par 4	Par 3	Par 4	Par 5	Par 3	Par 4	Par 36

HOW TO GET THERE

Alyth lies 5 miles north-east of Blairgowrie on the A926.

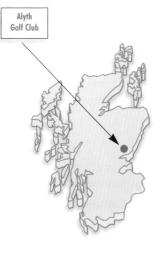

Alyth Golf Club

Blairgowrie

B lairgowrie Golf Club's Rosemount course is popular with visitors. Those who have played the links at Carnoustie and St Andrews often turn towards Blairgowrie and the pine-lined fairways of its Rosemount course to enjoy one of the country's finest inland tracts.

There is nothing dramatic about the course; in fact, after the wilds of links courses, some might find it a little demure. Tucked away with perfectly trimmed, pine avenues in a moorland setting, it is pristine and well-ordered in every way.

As with so many Scottish courses, James Braid had much to do with the design. The first four holes are hedged with heavy heather and pine, the 1st green with a tight entrance, while the 5th

opens out – slightly. The most memorable holes are perhaps the closing with the 16th being one of those psychological pickles, slightly uphill, out of bounds down the left and a stand of trees in the middle distance. On the outer limits of a Par 4, it needs a good tee shot to play this hole effectively.

The 17th is a Par 3 over a wide gully with a fine, two-tiered green. Plays long and, at worst, hope for assistance from the back-banking otherwise there is bitter adversity for the short shot.

The 18th is a good driving hole with most danger from the copse of trees on the right. There are yawning cross-bunkers ahead of the green but these should not come into play if you have driven well.

COURSE INFORMATION & FACILITIES

Blairgowrie Golf Club
Rosemount
Blairgowrie PH10 6LG

Managing Secretary: John N. Simpson.
Tel: 01250 872622. Fax: 01250 875451.

Golf Professional Tel: 01250 873116.

Green Fees:
Weekdays – £35. Weekends – £40.
Weekdays (day) – £48. Weekends (day) – £80.
Some time restrictions.

CARD OF THE COURSE – PAR 72									
1	2	3	4	5	6	7	8	9	Out
444	339	220	408	551	189	373	368	326	3218
Par 4	Par 4	Par 3	Par 4	Par 5	Par 3	Par 4	Par 4	Par 4	Par 35
10	11	12	13	14	15	16	17	18	In
507	500	293	401	512	129	475	165	390	3372
Par 5	Par 5	Par 4	Par 4	Par 5	Par 3	Par 4	Par 3	Par 4	Par 37

PERTHSHIRE

HOW TO GET THERE

From Aberdeen/Dundee: Turn left off Coupar Angust/Blairgowrie road. From Perth: Turn right off A93 on entering Rosemount.

KINLOCH HOUSE HOTEL
BY BLAIRGOWRIE · PERTHSHIRE PH10 6SG
TEL: 01250 884237 · FAX: 01250 884 333

David and Sarah Shentall welcome you to the Kinloch House Hotel. Built in 1840 and extended in 1911 with 21 bedrooms including two suites, most double and twin bedded rooms have a southerly aspect and all have private facilities with traditional furnishing to a very high standard.

Set in 25 acres of wooded policies and parkland with fine views to the south over Marlee Loch to the Sidlaw Hills beyond. There are some thirty or more golf courses within an hour's drive. The daily changing menus feature dishes created from fine Scottish produce skilfully prepared in our modern kitchen and recognised by the most profound guides.

 ★★★ ❀ ❀ ❀

55

Carnoustie

Carnoustie is a busy little Angus town and famous for golf. This corner of Scotland has contributed much to the game, sending native sons to all parts of the globe. But, despite this great reputation, few realise that there are actually three good courses at Carnoustie.

There is little need to mention the merits of the Carnoustie Championship course, home of the Open in 1999 and so many other famous events of the past. But it is the Burnside course that perhaps merits more attention. Intertwined with the famous 'sleeping giant', as the Championship course is often referred to, Burnside carries many of that course's characteristics but less of its length and intimidation.

As with the Championship, the Barry Burn comes into play on the Burnside, most notably on the Par 3, 5th, a hole that often plays into the prevailing wind with the burn to the right side of the green then turning across the front. With trees close in to the left, there is little left to chance off the tee here.

Other notable holes are the 14th, a longish Par 3 with an elevated green playing across a shallow valley and the Par 5, 15th. The 9th has a plateau green that is difficult to hold.

Most players will wish to take advantage of the excellent 'day ticket' that allows play on both Championship and Burnside courses for little more than the cost of one round on the Championship and when the Open returns to Carnoustie Championship in 1999, Burnside will be used as a qualifying course.

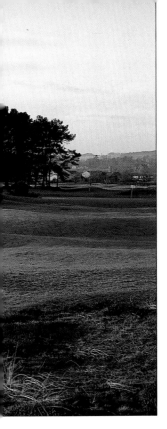

DUNDEE

COURSE INFORMATION & FACILITIES

Carnoustie Golf Links
Links Parade
Carnoustie DD7 7JE.

Secretary: E. J. C. Smith.
Tel: 01241 853789.
Fax: 01241 852720.

Green Fees:
Championship Course: £50.
Burnside Course: £18.
Buddon Links: £14.

CARD OF THE COURSE (Championship) – PAR 72

1	2	3	4	5	6	7	8	9	Out
401	435	337	375	387	520	394	167	413	3429
Par 4	Par 4	Par 4	Par 4	Par 4	Par 5	Par 4	Par 3	Par 4	Par 36
10	11	12	13	14	15	16	17	18	In
446	362	479	161	483	459	245	433	444	3512
Par 4	Par 4	Par 5	Par 3	Par 5	Par 4	Par 3	Par 4	Par 4	Par 36

HOW TO GET THERE

Course is situated at
Carnoustie, north east
rom Dundee.

Carnoustie
Golf Links

Crieff

rieff's Ferntower course is laid out over the hill above the rotunda pro-shop and the magnificent clubhouse. Just 17 miles from Perth and 10 miles north of Gleneagles, it is considered one of Perthshire's best courses.

It is an easy climbing course laid out in such a way that the inclines are gradual and the intent on the hole ahead foregoes any weariness in the legs. The clean, Highland air and uplifting views over the Strathearn Valley also help.

There are three Par 5's, two of them on the front nine and these sum up the nature of a round on the Ferntower. Tee shots are important throughout this course, both for accuracy and distance.

With lush, generous fairways and forgiving fringes, it is advisable to work with a driver otherwise the 6,400 yards of often-uphill lies, can prove rather stretching.

The 7th hole is from the original layout before John Stark extended the course in 1980. It is a long Par 4, usually playing into the wind and sloping right to left The green is fairly accommodating to allow for the hole's 454 yards. Stop here to appreciate the views back down to the valley.

The 12th is one of the newer holes, again, a long Par 4 of 467 yards with a soft dog-leg right, this time usually playing downwind and downhill so it is foreshortened but then this is a more difficult green, set into a conifer wood.

COURSE INFORMATION & FACILITIES

Crieff Golf Club – Ferntower Course
Ferntower
Perth Road, Crieff.

Managing Secretary: J. S. Miller.
Tel: 01764 652397. Fax: 01764 3803.

Golf Professional:
Tel: 01764 652397. Fax: 01764 655096.

Green Fees per 18 holes per day:
Weekdays – £19. Weekends – £26.
Weekdays (day) – £27. Weekends (day) – £35.

CARD OF THE COURSE – PAR 71

1	2	3	4	5	6	7	8	9	Out
163	380	418	124	532	482	454	303	511	3367
Par 3	Par 4	Par 4	Par 3	Par 5	Par 5	Par 4	Par 4	Par 5	Par 37
10	11	12	13	14	15	16	17	18	In
414	379	467	191	353	377	412	139	303	3035
Par 4	Par 4	Par 4	Par 3	Par 4	Par 4	Par 4	Par 3	Par 4	Par 34

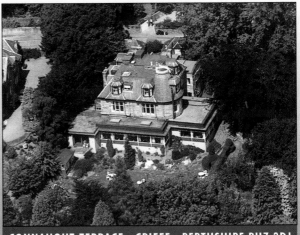
HOW TO GET THERE

Location: A85 15 miles to the west of
Perth on the main Perth-Crieff Road.
From the south take the M6 north,
leave at junction signposted
Braco Muthill, Crieff which
is 1 mile north of the
Dalhaldie Little Chef and
services.

Crieff
Golf Club

Downfield

Downfield Golf Club has consistently been rated as one of the finest inland courses in Scotland. Despite this, it isn't as well known as it should be and, perhaps because it is tucked out of the way a little, fewer touring golfers find their way there.

Chosen as a qualifying course for the 1999 Open at Carnoustie, its luxurious fairways will then, no doubt, be heaped with praise but anyone who wishes to savour a truly great parkland course beforehand should seek Downfield out.

James Braid laid out the original tract in an area now occupied by a 1960's housing development. In 1963, the present course was fashioned by one of the club members. Out of the original holes, the 10th, 11th and 12th still exist,

only slightly altered. Parts of the 15th and 16th are also of the Braid design but the rest of the course was built more recently.

The most challenging hole is the 4th, the greatest of the par 5's, with the Gelly Burn running diagonally across the fairway near the green. The 10th is a beautiful Par 4, 434 yards off the forward tee with a pond defending the green at around 40 yards out. A ditch, hidden between the pond and the green can mean double-trouble to those who don't know of its existence. Gary Player reckoned the 12th was one of the best par 3's he had ever seen, a short hole through the trees.

In a country know for its links courses, Downfield stands apart as one of the finest parklands.

COURSE INFORMATION & FACILITIES

Downfield Golf Club
Turnberry Avenue
Dundee DD2 3QP.

Secretary: Barrie D. Liddle.
Tel: 01382 825595. Fax: 01382 813111.

Golf Professional Tel: 01382 889246.

Green Fees:
Weekdays – £30. Weekends – £35.
Weekdays (day) – £45.
Some time restrictions.

CARD OF THE COURSE – PAR 73

1	2	3	4	5	6	7	8	9	Out
425	408	228	538	412	177	491	407	414	3500
Par 4	Par 4	Par 3	Par 5	Par 4	Par 3	Par 5	Par 4	Par 4	Par 36
10	11	12	13	14	15	16	17	18	In
434	498	182	480	515	326	352	151	384	3372
Par 4	Par 5	Par 3	Par 5	Par 5	Par 4	Par 4	Par 3	Par 4	Par 37

HOW TO GET THERE

From Dundee Ring Road (Kingsway) take exit at A923 Coupar Angus Road. At next roundabout take right turn into Faraday Street then first left into Harrison Road. Up hill and turn left at T-Junction. Follow Dalmahoy Drive for approx. 400 yards then take sharp turn left into Downfield Golf Club.

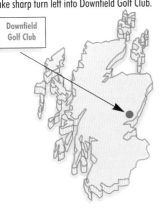

Downfield
Golf Club

Dunkeld & Birnam

Dunkeld is another focal point in the historic and scenic fabric of Perthshire. It was the centre of Scottish ecclesiastical life in the ninth century and now its ancient Cathedral remains, set in spacious parkland leading down to the River Tay.

A scenic 9-hole golf course is found high above the town with marvellous views of Birnam Hill and the Loch of Lowes to the east. The 3rd presents a deserving challenge on a moderate climb with rough and fields to the left and a distinct lean of the fairway towards this. Nearer the green stands a defensive rocky outcrop, which must be cleared with a sturdy second stroke to reach the blind green; not an easy task. Once you have delivered yourself from this dogged test, no matter what the outcome, take a

minute to appreciate the view from this lofty outlook. Below is the remarkable Loch of Lowes where ospreys breed each year, zealously watched over by the RSPB and many bird-watchers who visit the public hide. On the course, there are several wide gullies to cross and hills to ascend but each hole is a peach to play. The 5th is an easy Par 4 if you make landfall across the broad chasm.

The 7th plays over the access road and up one more slope while the green stays hidden upon another crest. Again, the advantage goes to a sound tee shot that clears the first precipice but, even then, it is a high lob with much danger before and aft the airy green. Dunkeld & Birnam Golf Club is part of the Highland Perthshire Ticket so play is possible here for an entire week for the price of, say a round of drinks at Gleneagles.

COURSE INFORMATION & FACILITIES

Dunkeld & Birnam Golf Club
Fungarth
Dunkeld, Perthshire.

Secretary: Mrs. W. A. Sinclair.
Tel: 01350 727564.
Fax: 01350 728660.

Green Fees:
Weekdays – £11. Weekends – £16.
Weekdays (Day) – £13. Weekends (Day) – £22.

CARD OF THE COURSE – PAR 70

1	2	3	4	5	6	7	8	9	Out
249	265	375	373	238	271	338	193	122	2424
Par 4	Par 4	Par 4	Par 4	Par 4	Par 4	Par 4	Par 3	Par 3	Par 35

10	11	12	13	14	15	16	17	18	In
249	265	375	373	238	271	338	193	122	2424
Par 4	Par 4	Par 4	Par 4	Par 4	Par 4	Par 4	Par 3	Par 3	Par 35

HOW TO GET THERE

Leave A9 and proceed through Dunkeld. Turn right on to the A923 Blairgowrie Road. Golf course signposted at top of the hill.

Dunkeld & Birnam Golf Club

Edzell

Part of the appeal of a golfing holiday in Scotland is to truly get-away-from it-all into the magnificent landscapes that this country is so famous for.

Edzell Golf Club is set far enough away from the well-spiked trails around St Andrews, Carnoustie or Ayrshire yet is easily accessible within an hour's drive from St Andrews or Aberdeen.

Where the foothills of the Grampian Mountains merge into the Vale of Strathmore, Edzell Golf Club plays over a varying parkland/heathland terrain well blended with mature trees. The course sets out over notable rises, the fine turf delighting golfers who have not experienced it before. Edzell is renowned for the quality of turf on fairways and greens.

The course's rhythm is unlike most in that you are tested at the 2nd hole with a Par 4 of 446 yards. All that can be done here is ensure that you are warmed up and psychologically prepared before you play.

Paramount on the back nine is the 14th hole known as Maguba, a battle in the Boer War. This is an uphill Par 3, heavily guarded but try to avoid leaving a downhill putt on the sloping surface. There is OOB to the rear in the form of the old railway as well as to the right.

Edzell's course is a concord of all that nature offers in this part of the world, heather, and fir trees, squirrels, deer, pheasants and finches. The clubhouse, though much modified and extended, still retains all the character of its 100-year vintage.

COURSE INFORMATION & FACILITIES

The Edzell Golf Club
High Street, Edzell
Brechin, Tayside DD9 7TF.

Secretary: Ian Farquhar
Tel: 01356 647283. Fax: 01356 648094.

Golf Professional:
Tel: 01356 648462.

Green Fees:
Weekdays – £20. Weekends – £26.
Weekdays (Day) – £30. Weekends (Day) – £39.

CARD OF THE COURSE – PAR 71

1	2	3	4	5	6	7	8	9	Out
312	446	310	370	429	178	385	354	478	3262
Par 4	Par 4	Par 4	Par 4	Par 4	Par 3	Par 4	Par 4	Par 5	Par 36

10	11	12	13	14	15	16	17	18	In
369	433	361	415	155	338	316	191	508	3086
Par 4	Par 4	Par 4	Par 4	Par 3	Par 4	Par 4	Par 3	Par 5	Par 35

HOW TO GET THERE

Travelling 1 mile north of Brechin on A94 take B966 left to Edzell. Continue for 3 miles to Edzell village. Club entrance is just beyond arch on entering village.

The Edzell Golf Club

Forfar

*T*he enduring memory most golfers leave Forfar Golf Club with, is of the greatly undulating fairways that they have negotiated.

Situated many miles from the sea, Forfar Golf Club was used for the drying of flax and the rolling swells that now cross many fairways are resultant from this process. Meanwhile, a rich growth of conifer and larch trees form the avenues that are Forfar's other main characteristic.

James Braid was responsible for the present course layout in 1926. The 6,000 yards are admirably carved in 80 acres and, surprisingly; there are no crossovers or fairways running too close.

On the front nine, the outstanding hole is the 5th, a Par 3 with its tee set back into the trees. It is a long carry with a menacing bank of gorse ahead of the green. Most use a 3 or 4-iron to avoid the penalties of landing short.

The 12th is a tough Par 4 where three good shots are needed to get on. Slightly dog-legged left with well-bunkered fairways, the need for accuracy prevails to a difficult sloping green.

Beware of unfair bounces that can come off the ridges running up, for instance, the 14th fairway. The 15th, 'Braid's Best', is the signature hole, a dog-leg right, although not as long as 12th. With the green sitting on the side of a slope, the ideal shots to approach this are a fade off the tee and fade for the second.

If you can keep out of the trees and bunkers at Forfar, you should score well.

HOW TO GET THERE

eave the A90 at the Coupar
ngus Junction to Forfar.
ollow the road through Forfar
eeping straight on at both
ets of traffic lights. Take
rbroath Road A932 out of
orfar. Club is one mile further
n the right just past
e Auchter Forfar
unction.

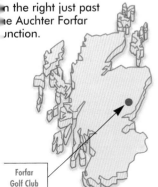

Forfar
Golf Club

COURSE INFORMATION & FACILITIES

Forfar Golf Club
Cunning Hill, Arbroath
Forfar DD8 2RL

Secretary: W. Baird.
Tel: 01307 463773. Fax: 01307 468495.

Golf Professional Tel: 01307 465683.

Green Fees:
Weekdays – £16. Weekends – £20.
Weekdays (day) – £24. Weekends (day) – £32.

CARD OF THE COURSE – PAR 69

1	2	3	4	5	6	7	8	9	Out
341	354	381	393	200	376	404	395	164	3008
Par 4	Par 4	Par 4	Par 4	Par 3	Par 4	Par 4	Par 4	Par 3	Par 34

10	11	12	13	14	15	16	17	18	In
359	352	444	154	478	412	153	344	348	3044
Par 4	Par 4	Par 4	Par 3	Par 5	Par 4	Par 3	Par 4	Par 44	Par 35

Killin

*T*here are still some real bargains to be found in the world of golf and the Perthshire Highland Ticket must be one of the best. For the price of one round on more expensive courses, you could have five days of golf on some of the most beautiful of Scotland's Highland gems.

Killin Golf Club is, arguably, the most beautiful of the five nine hole courses that participate in this programme, perched on the foothills of Ben Lawers and looking over the charming Highland village of the same name.

Apart from the Par 5, 9th of 514 yards off the back tee, none of the holes is long but there is plenty of interest in each. The 4th offers the trickiest test with a blind tee shot to the marker then a second blind shot to the green. A novel touch is the old hand-operated fire bell half way up the fairway to let the following group know you are clear.

The 5th is an 87-yard, par 3 with a dyke so close in front of the pin, it takes a very high lob to clear it and still hold the small green.

Coming back down to the floor of the course, the 9th is said to be one of the most scenic holes in Scotland with the dramatic Breadalbane Hills tranquil in the background. Once you have traversed this course you will relish going again. The Perthshire Highland Ticket is now structured so that you can play all your golf on the one course or sample any of the other nearby gems.

Killin Golf Club
Killin, Perthshire
FK21 8TY.

Secretary: J. R. Greaves
Tel: 01567 820705.

Club House:
Tel: 01567 820312.

Green Fees:
Weekdays – £12. Weekends – £12.
Weekdays (Day) – £15. Weekends (Day) – £15.

CARD OF THE COURSE – PAR 66

1	2	3	4	5	6	7	8	9	Out
288	211	206	361	97	327	340	159	519	2508
Par 4	Par 3	Par 3	Par 4	Par 3	Par 4	Par 4	Par 3	Par 5	Par 33

10	11	12	13	14	15	16	17	18	In
288	211	206	361	97	327	340	159	519	2508
Par 4	Par 3	Par 3	Par 4	Par 3	Par 4	Par 4	Par 3	Par 5	Par 33

m A9 Perth-Inverness Road – take A827 from
inluic through Aberfeldy and Kenmorg along Loch
– Golf Club on left as you drop into Killin. From M9
ling to Perth – exit Jct 10 (A84) to Callander and
hernhead. A85 Lochernhead to Crianlarich via Lix
. A827 Lix Toll turn right through Killin. Course on
it. From Oban (A85) or Fort
iam (A82) – take A85 to Tyndrum
182 to Tyndrum. Take A82 to
inlarich then A85 to Lix, turn
onto A827 at Lix –
ough Killin,
irse on
it.

Killin
Golf Club

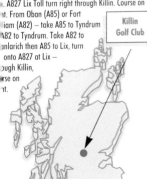

Kirriemuir

One of the most compact parcels of golfing land is to be found at the foot of the beautiful Angus Glens. Here, above the town of Kirriemuir, James Braid met the challenge of fitting 18 holes into just 77 acres. The result is a testing and entertaining heathland/parkland.

With an overall length of 5,550 yards, Kirrie is a fine length for most golfers with plenty variety on the front nine and some challenging tests on the tighter back.

The front seven holes play across open ground of a more parkland nature and, apart from some pines, do not pose too many problems.

It is the thicker vegetation of the back 9 that dogs the timid off the tees. There are trees, gorse, broom and heather along many of the fairways so accuracy as well as length is beneficial.

The finish at Kirriemuir has to be its most challenging aspect. The 17th is a long Par 3 with a couple of majestic trees on either side of the fairway. When in full bloom, they can get in the way if, in a wind, you want to start the ball left.

The 18th presents an uphill Par 4 with a blocking tree to the right and a massive gully just before the green. You would be happy to come off with par here.

COURSE INFORMATION & FACILITIES

Kirriemuir Golf Club
Northmuir, Kirriemuir
Angus DD8 4LN.

Director of Golf: Anthony Caira.
Tel: 01575 573317. Fax: 01575 574608.

Golf Professional:
Tel: 01575 573317. Fax: 01575 574608.

Green Fees per 18 holes per day:
Weekdays – £16. Weekdays (Day) – £22.

CARD OF THE COURSE – PAR 68

1	2	3	4	5	6	7	8	9	Out
373	147	414	335	277	384	301	154	352	2737
Par 4	Par 3	Par 4	Par 4	Par 4	Par 4	Par 4	Par 3	Par 4	Par 34

10	11	12	13	14	15	16	17	18	In
330	325	388	391	352	285	119	195	388	2773
Par 4	Par 4	Par 4	Par 4	Par 4	Par 4	Par 3	Par 3	Par 4	Par 34

HOW TO GET THERE

Situated to the north of Kirriemuir and easily accessible from main Dundee/Aberdeen dual carriageway (A94). Head into centre of town – follow one way system and turn left at "The Roods", continue right to top of road (2 miles) and you have arrived

Kirriemuir Golf Club

Panmure

anmure is a course that could be overlooked by golfers heading for the more conspicuous links at Carnoustie. And yet it is a course of great repute, full of Scottish golfing gusto and, having been involved with the development of the game since the 19th century, teeming with tradition.

On the course, it gets tight and tough especially in the summer months when the rough is high. Wind, as with all coastal courses, is another consideration.

For the first two holes, easy openers, there is little to remark on. The 3rd, 4th, and 5th offer more interest and are ideal warmers for the challenge to come.

The 6th is a classic in Scottish golf. A 387 yard, Par 4, there is little room for mistakes here. Off the tee, the ideal line may be left but there is a huge, safe landing area to the right where the 6th and 7th fairways merge.

Choosing this route has a major drawback. From here, it is a 4-iron or 3-wood to reach the elevated green and with the surrounding conditions as they are, only the greatest of good fortune would keep you from the heather and gorse or even worse, the railway line at the rear. The sole advice is to take an iron off the tee, stay as left as you dare and then you have a chance.

The rest of the course plays through some fascinating landscapes. Serpentine burn guards the 12th green while the 14th, well-bunkered all the way, needs two good strikes to see the green with a nasty old railway line to the right.

COURSE INFORMATION & FACILITIES

Panmure Golf Club
Barry, By Carnoustie
Angus DD7 7RT.

Secretary: Major Graeme Paton.
Tel: 01241 855120. Fax: 01241 859737.

Golf Professional:
Tel: 01241 852460. Fax: 01241 859737.

Green Fees:
Weekdays – £28. Weekends – £28.
Weekdays (day) – £42. Weekends (day) – £42.
Some time restrictions.

CARD OF THE COURSE – PAR 70

1	2	3	4	5	6	7	8	9	Out
289	488	398	348	147	387	418	360	174	3009
Par 4	Par 5	Par 4	Par 4	Par 3	Par 4	Par 4	Par 4	Par 3	Par 35
10	11	12	13	14	15	16	17	18	In
416	171	363	398	535	234	382	401	408	3308
Par 4	Par 3	Par 4	Par 4	Par 5	Par 3	Par 4	Par 4	Par 4	Par 35

HOW TO GET THERE

From the South and West: Follow A90 round Dundee to the last roundabout on the Kingsway. Follow A92 for Arbroath for about 1/2 miles. Turn right for Barry (T-junction). Continue straight over crossroads, turn right at first junction.
From the North: Follow A92 south of Arbroath, about miles after Muirdrum Village, turn left for Barry (T-junction), then as above.

Panmure Golf Club

Taymouth Castle

*D*riving through the gates of the Breadalbane Estate, the grey, castellated turrets of Taymouth Castle leap into view, surely an escape for a multi-millionaire or a world-class ' resort with its own golf course.

The location, castle and course certainly merit such a lofted status but, for humble touring golfers, they are certainly glad it remains down to earth and open to the travelling public.

Immediately to the west lies Loch Tay with the picturesque village of Kenmore at its mouth and the Tay, one of Scotland's most famous salmon rivers, beginning its sojourn east to the sea. Overlooking the loch and golf course is Ben Lawers and other smaller peaks but

it is the easternmost bowl of the valley, surrounded by woods and frequented by deer, on which the course is formed. The golfing terrain is, therefore, relatively flat.

James Braid designed the course in the 1920's. Braid's policy of leading players gently into the arena before testing them, holds true here with two short par 4's, a longer one then a delightful Par 3 at the 4th. The 5th is a demanding Par 5 of 543 yards and from there the contest is on.

Generally, the fairways are generous but the configuration and length make it challenging enough for a good golfer. Should a ball go off-line, the wispy rough can make it disappear into the fringe, never to be found again.

COURSE INFORMATION & FACILITIES

Taymouth Castle Golf Club
Taymouth Castle, Kenmore
Perthshire PH15 2NJ.

Director of Golf: Ian Stark.
Tel: 01887 830228. Fax: 01887 830765.

Golf Professional:
Alex Marshall.

Green Fees per 18 holes per day:
Weekdays – £17. Weekends – £21.
Weekdays (Day) – £28. Weekends (Day) – £38.

CARD OF THE COURSE – PAR 69/72

1	2	3	4	5	6	7	8	9	Out
296	306	420	170	543	365	283	383	377	3143
Par 4	Par 4	Par 4	Par 3	Par 5	Par 4	Par 4	Par 4	Par 4	Par 36

10	11	12	13	14	15	16	17	18	In
182	452	444	298	190	410	174	330	443	2923
Par 3	Par 4	Par 4	Par 4	Par 3	Par 4	Par 3	Par 4	Par 4	Par 33

HOW TO GET THERE

Follow A9 Inverness road through Perth. Turn off 5 miles south of Pitlochry, following Aberfeld signs follow road through Aberfeld heading for Killin. Golf Course is 5 miles out of Aberfeld.

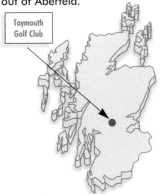

Taymouth
Golf Club

Grampian

Grampian

*T*he Grampian region is synonymous with castles, fishing and whisky. From Stonehaven, through Royal Deeside and north to the Moray Firth, the area embodies many of the elements that Scotland is famed for. As a golf destination it has renowned venues such as Royal Aberdeen and Cruden Bay, two of the most distinctive examples of links golf. Royal Aberdeen's front nine has long been recognised as one of the finest collections of outward holes while Cruden Bay, with its wild, sea dunes and dramatic setting, captures the heart of every earnest golfer. Recently, the area has launched an initiative to highlight the large selection of golf opportunities in addition to these two prime candidates. With currently 25 golf establishments participating in the project as well as some of the best hotels and golf holiday companies, the Grampian Golf Classics campaign is highlighting the area's many diverse golfing facets. Royal Deeside has long been an escape from the pell-mell of daily life and it was Queen Victoria who brought its invigorating environment to the attention of rest of the world. Today, the Royal Family still considers Balmoral as their main retreat from the pressures of court and capital. The consequent world-wide attention has, by no means, detracted from the area's attraction and visitors still enjoy the peace and tranquillity that existed here much as it must have in the Victorian era. With splendid accommodation and a wealth of fine eating establishments, Royal Deeside is complete for any visitor. For the golfer, it is therefore doubly rewarding. From Braemar in the west to the outskirts of Aberdeen, there are a dozen courses of the uppermost standard set in one of the most beautiful valleys in Scotland. The city of Aberdeen has become one of Europe's great centres and is still thriving after years of the North Sea oil boom. Industry has brought business people from all over the world that have discovered the golfing bounty that lies throughout this area and within the city. On the city's outskirts, Westhill Golf Club offers special packages for the *visiting businessman or tourist while facilities such as King's Links Golf Centre can fine tune a player's swing with a host of modern teaching equipment and the most skilled teaching professionals. The northeast coast around Peterhead and Fraserburgh is often uncharted territory for golfers but they are missing some testing links. Further east, the going gets a little easier although the Alistair Mackenzie greens at Duff House Royal will make up for any easy scoring on the wide fairways. Inland, Grampian is equally blessed but there is one hazard you might have not anticipated. This is whisky country and most of Scotland's distillers are found in the valley of the River Spey. With a free dram on offer at many of these establishments, driving of any kind can become a rather unsteady affair. The Grampian Golf Classics Ticket allows 5 days golf on a range of participating courses at greatly reduced green fees, during weekdays. A3-day ticket is also available. For more details on the Grampian Golf Classics ticket, telephone 01224 632727 or fax 01224 848805*

BALLATER
CRUDEN BAY
DUFF HOUSE ROYAL

MURCAR
NEWMACHAR
TARLAND

Ballater

*I*n the Victorian rush to discover and explore everything Scottish, Ballater Golf Club was founded in 1892. Originally a nine hole course, it was in 1905 that land became available to construct a further nine holes and the following year, a commemorative match was staged between the two notables of the time, James Braid and Harry Vardon.

Built in a bowl of the River Dee and surrounded by some glorious hillsides, Ballater is protected from bad weather and enjoys its own microclimate. 40 miles away in Aberdeen it can be pouring rain while Ballater is bone dry.

The course looks quite flat from the clubhouse but treading the fairways reveals subtle rolls and humps that can interfere with a well-struck ball. It is a fair test of golf but what it lacks in challenge it makes up in beauty.

The par 3, 5th stands as one of the best holes in golf in this region if not all of Scotland. With a large bunker on the front right and a ten-foot drop along the left, you have to hit the green and stay otherwise it could take a 4, 5 or even a 6 to get down.

Ballater, with its royal neighbours, is also a great place to dine. Per head of population there are more good eating-houses here than anywhere else in Britain.

COURSE INFORMATION & FACILITIES

Ballater Golf Club
Victoria Road
Aberdeenshire AB35 5QX.

Secretary: A. E. Barclay.
Tel: 013397 55567. Fax: 013397 55567.

Golf Professional: Frank Smith
Tel: 013397 55658

Green Fees:
Weekdays – £17. Weekends – £20.
Weekdays (day) – £26. Weekends (day) – £30.

CARD OF THE COURSE – PAR 67

1	2	3	4	5	6	7	8	9	Out
394	413	180	409	177	338	457	324	208	2900
Par 4	Par 4	Par 3	Par 4	Par 3	Par 4	Par 4	Par 4	Par 3	Par 33

10	11	12	13	14	15	16	17	18	In
375	420	365	157	310	337	318	153	303	2738
Par 4	Par 4	Par 4	Par 3	Par 4	Par 4	Par 4	Par 3	Par 4	Par 34

HOW TO GET THERE

On A93 approx. 42 miles west of Aberdeen. Turn left in village at Victoria Road, proceed to the very end.

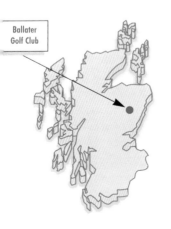

Ballater
Golf Club

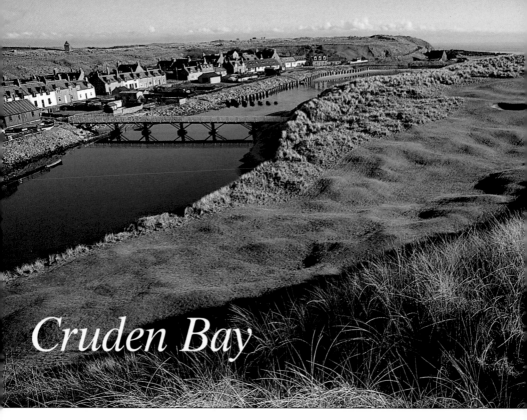

Cruden Bay

ruden Bay is one of the most extravagant links golf courses in the world, great carbuncles of marran-crested sand dunes interspersed with irresistible patches of velvet green.

Beyond the dunes lies the Bay of Cruden and the North Sea. It was here, in 1899, that the Great North of Scotland Railway Company chose to build the 'Gleneagles of the North', a hotel and golf complex that was sadly discarded in the 1930's.

Fortunately, Cruden Bay golf course lives on and is now one of the most popular courses in Scotland. From the 1st tee, the line is off the distant outline of Slains Castle, inspiration for Bram Stoker's Dracula.

Topping the headland a mile or so away, its eerie silhouette dominates the course but for the first three holes it proves a useful reference point.

Turning towards the sea, the 4th is a Par 3 of 193 yards, very demanding especially into the wind and one of the most beautiful settings for a golf hole. The Water of Cruden runs along its left side with the delightful old fishing village of Cruden Bay on the opposite bank.

Cruden Bay is not a long course with a standard scratch of 70 which is perhaps a couple of shots on the low side for championship tournaments but it makes up for those two shots by being quite tricky in places especially when there is wind – and when isn't there! It is a course that has fans from every part of the world and this is quite understandable.

COURSE INFORMATION & FACILITIES

Cruden Bay Golf Club
Aulton Road
Peterhead AB42 0NN.

Secretary/Manager:
Mrs. Rosemary Pittendrigh.
Tel: 01779 812285. Fax: 01779 812945.

Golf Professional:
Tel: 01779 812414. Fax: 01779 812414.

Green Fees:
Weekdays (day) – £30. Weekends (day) – £40.

CARD OF THE COURSE – PAR 70

1	2	3	4	5	6	7	8	9	Out
416	339	286	193	454	529	392	258	462	3329
Par 4	Par 4	Par 4	Par 3	Par 4	Par 5	Par 4	Par 4	Par 4	Par 36
10	11	12	13	14	15	16	17	18	In
385	149	320	550	397	239	182	428	416	3066
Par 4	Par 3	Par 4	Par 5	Par 4	Par 3	Par 3	Par 4	Par 4	Par 34

HOW TO GET THERE

Cruden Bay is some 25 miles north of Aberdeen, lying on the coast about five miles below Peterhead.

Cruden Bay
Golf Club

Duff House Royal

*A*cross the seven-arched bridge of the River Deveron is Duff House Royal Golf Club. It is the most noted course in the area and the same designer as those of Augusta National, Dr Alistair McKenzie, created its greens. Set within the bounds of the course, Duff House is a Georgian Baroque mansion recently refurbished and opened as a country house art gallery.

Duff House's course is close to the sea but it is pure parkland, flat and easy to walk. It is renowned for its lush fairways and large bunkers but it is the greens that stand out and it is here you need to be careful. Most are exceptionally large and at least double tiered, as was Dr McKenzie's caprice back in the 1920's. Once you have sampled them you learn it is often better to play short and chip rather than leave lengthy, risky putts. The greens, however, are not fast. It is their size that is the challenge. The 16th is a good example, a long Par 3 of 242 yards where it is reasonable to play short and putt on using a 7 iron.

There are three large bunkers on the left and the River Deveron to the right posing threats but the movement on the green and a distinct slope towards the bunker side dictate a safe approach.

The 12th plays toward Duff House, the only hole without a bunker, a Par 5 with a large, high-plateau green that is very difficult to hit and hold.

COURSE INFORMATION & FACILITIES

Duff House Royal Golf Club
The Barnyards
Banff AB45 3SX

Administrator: Mrs. Jan Corbett.
Tel: 01261 812062. Fax: 01261 812224.

Golf Professional Tel: 01261 812075.

Green Fees:
Weekdays – £16. Weekends – £20.
Weekdays (Day) – £23. Weekends (Day) – £28.

CARD OF THE COURSE – PAR 68

1	2	3	4	5	6	7	8	9	Out
314	366	392	367	330	139	460	381	172	2921
Par 4	Par 4	Par 4	Par 4	Par 4	Par 3	Par 4	Par 4	Par 3	Par 34

10	11	12	13	14	15	16	17	18	In
403	214	498	175	434	468	242	462	344	3293
Par 4	Par 3	Par 5	Par 3	Par 4	Par 4	Par 3	Par 4	Par 4	Par 34

HOW TO GET THERE

Located on Moray Firth
Coast approximately
50 miles from Aberdeen
on the A947.

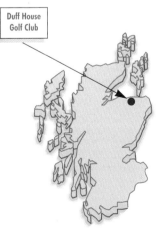

Duff House
Golf Club

Murcar

*I*n the pro-shop at Murcar Golf Club, there is a weather barometer showing current conditions and players are advised to stand before it for a minute to prepare them for conditions ahead.

It is no exaggeration to say that, like all Scottish links courses, conditions in the air are as germane to your game as the situation on the ground. This course is no monster in length but, on most days, it is all about driving the ball with or against or through the wind.

From the 1st tee, Murcar does not look too terrible, a fairly easy Par 4. The 2nd is similar but turning down into the folds of dunes at the 3rd, the temperament of the course changes.

Adjacent to the 10th tee of its

neighbour, Royal Aberdeen, the 3rd, a Par 4 of nearly 400 yards, throws up some volcanic bumps and grizzly gorse along its way and introduces you to the disposition of the next few holes.

With most of the holes here, the greens are sanctuaries you are so glad to gain. The 7th is a fine example, a raised tee looking over to the sea with two burns crossing the fairway down below, both within driving reach. It is the green-side dunes that alarm, a large carbuncle precluding safe entry and further assisted by two green-side bunkers.

The overall feel of Murcar is that it is quite difficult but it will give way to those that can play in the wind and are not over ambitious with the driver.

COURSE INFORMATION & FACILITIES

Murcar Golf Club
Bridge of Don
Aberdeen AB23 8BD.

Secretary: R. Matthews.
Tel: 01224 704354. Fax: 01224 704354.

Golf Professional Tel: 01224 704370.

Green Fees:
Weekdays – £28. Weekends – £43.
Weekdays (day) – £38. Weekends (day) – £43.
Handicap certificates required.

CARD OF THE COURSE – PAR 71

1	2	3	4	5	6	7	8	9	Out
322	367	401	489	162	439	423	383	312	3298
Par 4	Par 4	Par 4	Par 5	Par 3	Par 4	Par 4	Par 4	Par 4	Par 36

10	11	12	13	14	15	16	17	18	In
395	338	152	383	476	351	160	359	329	2943
Par 4	Par 4	Par 3	Par 4	Par 5	Par 4	Par 3	Par 4	Par 4	Par 35

HOW TO GET THERE

Approx 5 miles from centre of Aberdeen to N.E. off A92 Peterhead/Fraserburgh Road.

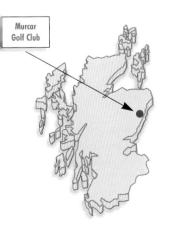

Murcar
Golf Club

Newmachar

Newmachar Golf Club is a fairy story of how one man, local police sergeant, Charlie Keith, had a dream of a golf course closer to his village and the reality, some 12 years later, has, no doubt, well surpassed his original vision.

Now with two exceptional 18-hole layouts, a magnificent clubhouse and one of the largest practice/teaching facilities in Scotland, Newmachar is one of the main golf complexes in the northeast.

Only 15 minutes from Aberdeen city centre and 10 minutes from Aberdeen's Dyce Airport, it is in a prime position to be included on a tour of the area's premier courses including Royal Aberdeen and Cruden Bay.

The Hawkshill course, designed by Dave Thomas, is the original and a much-varied test of every element of the game. Several holes resemble US style courses with water carries being the prominent hazard.

But it is the woodland holes, more akin to Rosemount or Gleneagles, that offer most pleasure with many tight drives and tricky turns. Unless each stoke is played judiciously, this can be a trying examination for every level of player.

As testament to the calibre of the Hawkshill, the Scottish Seniors Open has recently been held here and is scheduled to return. The new Swailend course is a wider, rolling and altogether easier test but, at 6,300 yards and with over 15,000 trees planted, there is still plenty room for challenge.

COURSE INFORMATION & FACILITIES

Newmachar Golf Club
Swailend, Newmachar
Aberdeen AB21 7UU

Manager: George A. McIntosh.
Tel: 01651 863002. Fax: 01651 863055.

Golf Professional Tel: 01651 862127.

Green Fees: Hawkshill Course
Weekdays – £25. Weekends – £30.
Weekdays (day) – £35. Weekends (day) – £40.
Letter of introduction required.

CARD OF THE COURSE – PAR 72

1	2	3	4	5	6	7	8	9	Out
390	543	331	378	320	170	405	493	181	3211
Par 4	Par 5	Par 4	Par 4	Par 4	Par 3	Par 4	Par 5	Par 3	Par 36

10	11	12	13	14	15	16	17	18	In
337	381	428	399	362	210	504	432	359	3412
Par 4	Par 4	Par 4	Par 4	Par 4	Par 3	Par 5	Par 4	Par 4	Par 36

HOW TO GET THERE

12 miles north of Aberdeen off main A947.
Aberdeen/Banff Road – which is signposted.

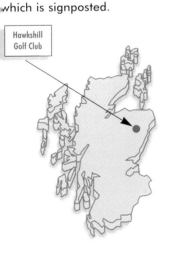

Hawkshill Golf Club

Tarland

Tarland Golf Club, set on the northern slopes of the Dee Valley, is only nine holes and appears quite elementary on a score card map. Playing over the course is an entirely different experience. Each of its nine holes offers a different golfing encounter.

The 1st is an easy start but not without its hazards, either from a fade that rolls into the rough to the right or by playing a second shot too long over the green and into the large, waiting bunker.

It is the 4th and 5th holes that are the most notable on this course. At a stretch of the imagination, the 4th has shades of Augusta with a burn and bridge crossing before a pine-surrounded green.

The 5th is a long Par 3 of 238 yards with high trees infringing on the left and a rough road and more trees to the right so this is a very demanding shot.

The remaining holes travel back and forth on a more open area but there is plenty adventure in each of them.

The course records stands at only one under Par so this gives some indication of the calibre of the club. Good golfers enjoy it and average golfers are happy with the easy walking and lovely views.

Part of the attraction at Tarland, although by no means a measure of its quality, is the extraordinarily cheap cost of a day's golf. For the price of a glove, you can play till your heart's content. The little clubhouse is very friendly, comfortable and serves good meals through the season.

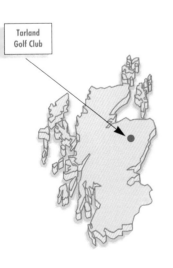

COURSE INFORMATION & FACILITIES

Tarland Golf Club
Aberdeen Road
Tarland, Aboyne

Secretary:
Raymond Reid.
Tel: 013398 81413.

Green Fees:
Weekdays (day) – £12.
Weekends (day) – £15.

CARD OF THE COURSE – PAR 66

1	2	3	4	5	6	7	8	9	Out
309	350	171	373	236	450	172	437	398	2896
Par 4	Par 4	Par 3	Par 4	Par 3	Par 4	Par 3	Par 4	Par 4	Par 33
10	11	12	13	14	15	16	17	18	In
311	350	221	379	208	415	211	486	398	2979
Par 4	Par 4	Par 3	Par 4	Par 3	Par 4	Par 3	Par 4	Par 4	Par 33

HOW TO GET THERE

North off the A93 –
Royal Deeside Route

Tarland
Golf Club

Highlands & Islands

Highlands & Islands

*C*rossing the great, mountainous barrier of the Drumochter Pass into the Highland region, there is a feeling of entering another country, quite separate from the lowlands to the south. With the mighty Grampian and Cairngorm Mountains as their defence and boundary, the Highlands were partly cut off from the rest of Scotland for many centuries. In this way, it developed its own character and culture which survives today. The golf courses here are also unique, embodying the scenery and constitution of the land on which they are built. Following the A9 or Great North Road from the south, the Victorian towns of Newtonmore and Kingussie appear nestled beneath the Monadhliath Mountains. Not only are these ideal golf destinations but they are relaxing and revitalising Highland communities in their own right, worth spending time to become aquatinted with. A little further north is the renowned Boat of Garten Golf Club, perhaps the course that best captures the essence of Highland golf. Here, from the 2nd tee, the view is fairly breathtaking. Grantown-on-Spey is another excellent test while Carrbridge and Nethybridge offer two holiday layouts that are by no means easy. The town of Inverness is a good base for touring the Highlands with Loch Ness, Urquhart Castle and many more attractions all within easy driving distance. Inverness Golf Club is a plush parkland overlooking the town and the Beauly Firth. East of Inverness is the town of Nairn, referred to as the 'Brighton of the North' because of its warm climate. Here are two excellent tests, the Nairn Golf Club being the venue for 1999's Walker Cup. North of Inverness, the golf courses form a chain along the coast that makes for an ideal golf-tour itinerary. These include Fortrose and Rosemarkie, Tain, Royal Dornoch, Golspie and Brora. The Carnegie Club at Dornoch also offers one of the best new courses in Scotland however it is mainly for the guests of Skibo Castle and otherwise rather expensive. Further north, John o' Groats beckons with courses at nearby Reay and Wick. It is the Northern Isles of Orkney and Shetland that offer surprisingly good links, some such as at Whalsay, the most northerly in the UK, and a must for the true golf course bagger. The most northerly course on the mainland is found at Durness near Cape Wrath on the northwest corner. The West Coast of the Highlands does not offer so much golf, just the most spectacular scenery you have probably ever seen. However, it is worth seeking out Gairloch Golf Club near the town of the same name. Traigh Golf Club on the road to the Isles is also worth diverting for if you are approaching Skye via that route. The Isle of Skye and the Western Isles have several fine courses, ideal if you have come to this region for their many attractions and wish to play. The holiday capital of Fort William, sheltered under towering Ben Nevis offers golf at Fort William Golf Club or Spean Bridge. Island golf may not be hugely popular but many are happy to keep it that way. The views from Barra, Colonsay or Tiree over the Atlantic Ocean and their deserted beaches is enough to make a keen hacker drop his clubs and just stare. Further south, the island of Islay has one of Scotland's most special links that many golfers make a special effort to reach. Machrie is an archetypal links that lingers as long as the aftertaste of Islay's superlative single malts. For more details on golfing in the Highlands of Scotland contact the Highlands of Scotland Tourist Board on 0990 143070.

BOAT OF GARTEN	KINGUSSIE
BRORA	NAIRN DUNBAR
DURNESS	NEWTONMORE
FORTROSE & ROSEMARKIE	ROYAL DORNOCH
GOLSPIE	STRATHPEFFER
MACHRIE – ISLAY	TAIN

Boat of Garten

The Boat of Garten Golf Club has a reputation, which it admirably upholds, of possessing one of the most breathtaking settings of any course in Scotland. It also adds the nostalgic touch of the Strathspey Steam Railway running along its western flank.

The view from the 2nd tee includes the craggy peaks of the Cairngorm Mountains acting as its backdrop to the green. Its fairway bends from the tee to a mildly sloping green.

For the first three holes, the "Boat" is relatively plain sailing but, despite the waft of pine and heather and the evocative smell of steam trains, the 4th may make you feel a little queasy. All the way to the putting surface, one of the Boat of Garten's most notable features comes into play. Wild undulations intersect the fairway causing havoc with rolling balls.

The 6th fairway is lined with pine and birch and turns right towards the green. There is no way through the trees, only forward to drop the ball within striking distance of the green. Another tight 200 yards will get you home but the green can toss the ball over its lumpy back and off down a steep-sided bank.

After this hole, it pays to settle and enjoy the scenery, which is peerless. From the height of the 12th tee there is a fine view south and the River Spey can be looked down upon from the 14th tee. The Boat's closing hole is one of the most formidable. In a wind it can require two mighty blows to come near to the elevated green which is very difficult to hit and hold.

Boat of Garten lies east of the A9, 5 miles north of Aviemore and is well signposted from the main road.

Boat of Garten
Golf Club

COURSE INFORMATION & FACILITIES

Boat of Garten Golf Club
Inverness-shire
PH24 3BQ

Secretary: Paddy Smyth.
Tel: 01479 831282. Fax: 01479 831523.

Golf Professional Tel: 01479 831282.

Green Fees:
Weekdays (day) – £20. Weekends (day) – £25.
Handicap certificates required.

CARD OF THE COURSE – PAR 69

1	2	3	4	5	6	7	8	9	Out
188	360	163	514	333	403	386	355	154	2856
Par 3	Par 4	Par 3	Par 5	Par 4	Par 4	Par 4	Par 4	Par 3	Par 34

10	11	12	13	14	15	16	17	18	In
271	379	349	432	323	307	168	344	437	3010
Par 4	Par 4	Par 4	Par 4	Par 4	Par 4	Par 3	Par 4	Par 4	Par 35

Brora

Brora is known as a brisk course, both for its breezes and the speed of play it enjoys. Little shelter is found for the cows and sheep that are allowed to wander the fairways and the same applies to golfers who tend to march smartly around this course in old Scottish style.

It was Old Tom Morris who established the original few holes here in 1891 while, in the 1920's, James Braid upgraded the links, maintaining a traditional character with little rough or man-made hazards and allowing the natural aspects of the land to come forward into play.

On this true links layout, there is a certain flavour of St Andrews Old Course with prescribed routes offering the best green approach. On the 12th, a drive down the right of the undulating fairway will flirt with OOB but leave a more positive view of the green.

The 9th is one of the most visually rewarding with the green terminating just before the beach and bay with the hills of Sutherland in the background. The greens, which are always in such supreme condition, are surrounded by electric fences used to protect them from the grazing animals.

This was Braid's most northerly course and the town of Brora and more specifically, the Royal Marine Hotel in Golf Road, is the base of the James Braid Golfing Society. This organisation is dedicated to the memory and principles of the great player and course architect who includes Gleneagles, Carnoustie and Royal Musselburgh as his work as well as some 200 others.

COURSE INFORMATION & FACILITIES

Brora Golf Club
Golf Road, Brora
Sutherland KW9 6QS.

Secretary: James Fraser.
Tel: 01408 621417.

Golf Professional Tel: 01408 621473.

Green Fees:
Weekdays – £18. Weekends – £18.
Weekdays (day) – £24. Weekends (day) – £24.

CARD OF THE COURSE – PAR 69

1	2	3	4	5	6	7	8	9	Out
297	344	447	325	428	174	350	501	162	3028
Par 4	Par 4	Par 4	Par 4	Par 4	Par 3	Par 4	Par 5	Par 3	Par 35

10	11	12	13	14	15	16	17	18	In
435	412	362	125	334	430	345	438	201	3082
Par 4	Par 4	Par 4	Par 3	Par 4	Par 4	Par 4	Par 4	Par 3	Par 34

HOW TO GET THERE

rora is situated on main A9
1 miles north of Inverness.
e golf course is on the coast
the heart of the
lage. From the
uth turn right just
ver the bridge and
llow the river to the
each Car Park which
djoins
e Club
ouse.

| Brora Golf Course |

THE LINKS AND ROYAL MARINE HOTELS

- The Links and Royal Marine Hotels, adjacent to the sea and James Braid's 18 hole Brora Links course, are the perfect base for touring the Highlands.
- Newly constructed leisure club including heated indoor swimming pool, sauna and leisure facilities.
- Variety of restaurants and bars.
- River, Loch and Sea Angling
- The Links View Apartments and Holiday Cottages available for let.

Highland Escape
The Links and Royal Marine Hotels
Golf Road, Brora, Sutherland KW9 6QS
Tel: 01408 621252 · Fax: 01408 621181
We have charged email address to: email highlandescape@btinternet.com

Durness

There are certain courses in Scotland which may only have nine holes, are far from the hubbub of modern life and may not present the stiffest of challenges. But they still sit very high on the 'must to be played' list.

At the northernmost corner of the Scottish mainland, Durness Golf Club is 300 miles from Edwardian elegance of Edinburgh and a short boat ride from Cape Wrath. You don't get much more remote than this but you also don't get much more beautiful.

It's a simple affair, nine holes carefully placed along the Faraid Head peninsula set behind the ancient Baloakeil Church, the most northern course on the Scottish mainland.

Just one of the wonderful things about Durness Golf Club, as well as most northerly Scottish courses, is that it can be light here well into the night. In fact, at the height of the summer, although it might be freezing and blowing a gale, the sun only really disappears between midnight and 2am.

This makes for some very pleasant evening rounds and Durness is one of the most fantastic courses to play at this time. Puffins and gannets are plentiful around this peninsula

The ultimate hole here and one of the most exciting anywhere must be the 9th or 18th, playing over the Atlantic Ocean.

COURSE INFORMATION & FACILITIES

Durness Golf Club
Balnakeil, Durness
Lairg, Sutherland IV27 4PN

Secretary: Lucy Mackay.
Tel: 01971 511364.

Green Fees:
Weekdays (day) – £12.
Weekends (day) – £12.

CARD OF THE COURSE – PAR 70

1	2	3	4	5	6	7	8	9	Out
296	321	408	287	344	443	178	377	108	2762
Par 4	Par 4	Par 4	Par 4	Par 4	Par 5	Par 3	Par 4	Par 3	Par 35
10	11	12	13	14	15	16	17	18	In
282	311	391	323	312	505	154	360	155	2793
Par 4	Par 4	Par 4	Par 4	Par 4	Par 5	Par 3	Par 4	Par 3	Par 35

HOW TO GET THERE

The club is 57 miles North West of Lairg on the A838.

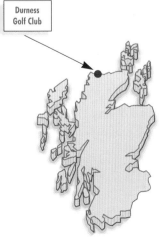

Durness Golf Club

CAPE WRATH HOTEL

How much further north can you get where hospitality reigns supreme?

Cape Wrath Hotel is situated less than a ten minute drive to Durness Golf Course which is amongst the top ten courses in the North of Scotland.
In one of the last truly unspoiled counties of Scotland, the Cape Wrath Hotel stands on a peninsula in the beautiful Kyle of Durness.
The Cape Wrath Hotel offers full facilities, excellent cuisine and warm welcome for all its guests.

Durness, Sutherland, Scotland
For reservations and enquiries Tel: (01971) 511212

Fortrose & Rosemarkie

*F*ortrose and Rosemarkie Golf course covers a thin, wizened peninsula jutting out from the Black Isle into the Moray Firth. This is a picturesque and pastoral part of Scotland but the course presents some vigorous challenges.

The beach and water surrounding the course are not 'out of bounds' and a single-track road, also 'in bounds', dissects the course for its length. You play the ball as it lies on these hazards or lift and drop for a penalty stroke.

When Fortrose and Rosemarkie looks lovely and docile beware of that snarling tiger, the wind. There are only two holes that go with or against it, the 9th and the 5th, while the rest are crossed by the prevailing south-westerlies.

Although it is put down as a traditional Scottish links course there are not many of what you would call 'links holes'. The 4th is most typical and a very good hole with links type undulations. The 17th is an excellent driving hole with restricting bunkers on the left and a jungle of rough and whins on the right. The main difficulty throughout the course is the small greens.

At the tip of Chanonry Point, just beyond the golf course, stands a memorial stone to the legendary Brahan Seer who was burned in a barrel of oil here for revealing too much detail of the Count of Seaforth's extra-marital activities. The Point provides one of the best places to see the Moray Firth's school of bottlenose dolphins who regularly make an appearance.

HOW TO GET THERE

\9 north of Inverness to
ore Roundabout. A832 to
ortrose (east direction).
urn right at Fortrose Police
itation to Golf Club.

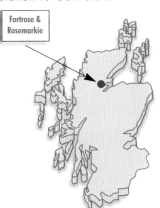

Fortrose &
Rosemarkie

COURSE INFORMATION & FACILITIES

Fortrose & Rosemarkie Golf Club
Ness Road East, Fortrose, Ross-Shire
Scotland IV10 8SE
Secretary/Treasurer: Margaret Collier.
Tel: 01381 620529.
Fax: 01381 620529.
Green Fees:
Weekdays – £16. Weekends – £22.
Weekdays (day) – £22. Weekends (day) – £30.
Some time restrictions.

CARD OF THE COURSE – PAR 71

1	2	3	4	5	6	7	8	9	Out
331	412	303	455	132	469	303	389	196	2990
Par 4	Par 4	Par 4	Par 5	Par 3	Par 5	Par 4	Par 4	Par 3	Par 36

10	11	12	13	14	15	16	17	18	In
322	381	394	308	267	293	336	355	212	2868
Par 4	Par 4	Par 4	Par 4	Par 4	Par 4	Par 4	Par 4	Par 3	Par 35

Golspie

If you would like to experience most of Scotland's golfing conditions, captured in one course, head for Golspie on the Sutherland coast, 10 miles north of Dornoch.

From the clubhouse, the course sets out as a pan-flat meadow, not quite parkland but of the same sort of loam. Then, at the 3rd, it turns back along the beach for a firm taste of links.

At the 6th you migrate toward the heathland section in Ferry Wood, a newer area that was laid out by James Braid in 1926. This is an attractive corner, surrounded by pine trees and heather rough. It comprises of the 8th, 9th and 10th. Visitors enjoy the contrast here although some complain of nervousness playing over the pond at the 10th.

Playing along the road on the 11th to the 14th is, once again, pastureland where the rough, sparse as it is, is all the harder to escape from. Then onto the final stretch which has the bumps and springy turf of links. The 16th is perhaps the most memorable of these, a short hole of 176 yards playing over a depression to a two tiered green with a sentinel bunker on the front left. There are several lengthy Par 4's on the card and one decent Par 5, the 4th, which plays along the beach. All of these are greatly enhanced by the wind and can prove genuine tests.

Golspie's 5, 800 yards can seem innocuous on a good day but, more often than not, the wind is coming off the sea or over the Sutherland hills turning Golspie into a much more weighty challenge.

CARD OF THE COURSE – PAR 68

1	2	3	4	5	6	7	8	9	Out
425	175	367	527	292	156	284	408	412	3046
Par 4	Par 3	Par 4	Par 5	Par 4	Par 3	Par 4	Par 4	Par 4	Par 35

10	11	12	13	14	15	16	17	18	In
148	345	338	329	425	420	177	217	445	2844
Par 3	Par 4	Par 4	Par 4	Par 4	Par 4	Par 3	Par 3	Par 4	Par 33

HOW TO GET THERE

0 miles north of Dornoch
and five miles south of Brora
n the A9. Five minute drive
rom the village (Golspie).
mple parking at the club

Golspie
Golf Club

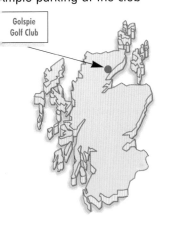

The Machrie

*T*he island of Islay may seem a rather remote place to travel for a round of golf but those that have will tell you it is an essential item in any serious golfer's education.

It is a unique experience in many ways. First of all you have to get there, which means a short flight to the island from Glasgow Airport or a 2-hour ferry crossing from Kennecraig on Kintyre to Port Ellen.

You then make your way to the Machrie Hotel, for previous visitors, a bastion of fine memories of evenings by the open fire in the bar sampling some after-dinner Islay malts – that is if they can remember anything about it at all.

The course is owned by and plays around the hotel, a wonderful example of a traditional Scottish links although, many would say, a course like no other.

Like a very shaggy dog that has broken out in a desperate case of green hives, Machrie is an exuberant piece of golf course architecture. The greens are placed in hollows and dells or on top of sand hills, very often out of sight of the tees or the fairways. For the first timer, it is a mystery tour, and if you are playing with a local, very much a case of following the leader.

One of the most impressive holes is the 'Scots Maiden' with a large dune immediately in front of the tee. Scenic views are all along the shoreline at the 2nd, 7th, 8th and 9th overlooking the seven-mile stretch of beach known as the Strand.

COURSE INFORMATION & FACILITIES

The Machrie Hotel & Golf Links
Port Ellen, Isle of Islay
Argyll PA42 7AN.

Manager: Mr Ian Brown.
Tel: 01496 302310.
Fax: 01496 302404.

Green Fees:
Weekdays – £17.50.
Weekdays (day) – £26.

CARD OF THE COURSE – PAR 71

1	2	3	4	5	6	7	8	9	Out
308	508	319	390	163	344	395	337	392	3156
Par 4	Par 5	Par 4	Par 4	Par 3	Par 4	Par 4	Par 4	Par 4	Par 36

10	11	12	13	14	15	16	17	18	In
156	357	174	488	423	335	411	352	374	3070
Par 3	Par 4	Par 3	Par 5	Par 4	Par 4	Par 4	Par 4	Par 4	Par 35

HOW TO GET THERE

plane from Glasgow Airport, flight time
0 minutes. By ferry from Kennacraig,
rgyll, crossing time 2 hours Glasgow is
bout 110 miles by road from Kennagraig.
he course is minutes from each terminal
urtesy coach will collect hotel
sidents.

The Machrie
Golf Club

The Machrie Hotel provides a warm and friendly service and
has the added advantage of having an inspiring golf course
on the doorstep.
With both superior and standard rooms and 15 twin bedroom
lodges, we can cater for both the individual golfer or larger
groups on a fully inclusive or self-catering basis.
With snooker, pool and croquet at the hotel and six operational
malt whisky distilleries on the island, and of course, the golf,
there is always something to do. For details of the hotel and
golfing packages available contact:
**The Machrie Hotel, Port Ellen, Isle of Islay PA42 7AN
Tel: 01496 302310 · Fax: 01496 302404**

Kingussie

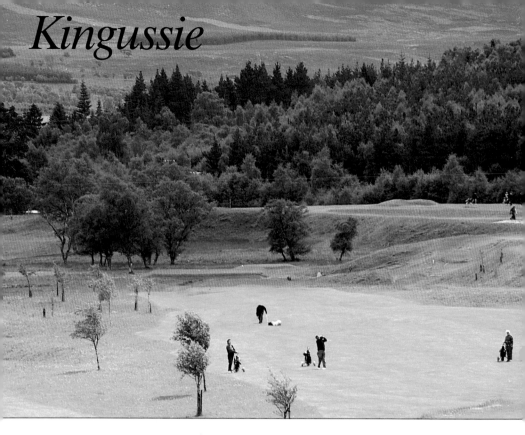

The Highlands of Scotland must be one of the most romantic places to come and golf and there are many splendid courses to choose from, all within a half-hour's drive of each other.

Kingussie Golf Club is particularly popular with holiday golfers. It is not overly demanding at only 5,555 yards yet there are one or two climbs either to elevated tees or high greens but it is the elevation and views over to the Cairngorms, with the sultry Monadhliath Mountains to the west, that give this course its appeal.

The name Kingussie is derived from Gaelic meaning 'the Head of the Pinewood' and it is out of the pinewoods and onto the foothills of the Monadhlaiths that Kingussie's fairways rise. Looking back from the 4th green you can take full advantage of the promontory so pack a camera. The following three holes play over this level so there is plenty time to admire the vista.

Kingussie suits most levels of golfer with fairly straight-forward fairways and room to recover a badly angled tee shot. The longer Par 4's are the most difficult but not overly so. Three of the six Par 3's cross the road and the Gynack Burn and are good fun especially the 15th at only 100 yards.

Kingussie's clubhouse has an air of conviviality and is well-worth becoming aquainted with after a round or for an evening meal.

Kingussie Golf Club
Kingussie
Inverness-shire PH21 1LR.

Secretary:
Norman MacWilliam.
Tel: 01540 661600. Fax: 01540 662066.

Green Fees:
Weekdays – £13.50. Weekends – £15.50.
Weekdays (Day) – £16.50. Weekends (Day) – £20.50.

CARD OF THE COURSE – PAR 66

1	2	3	4	5	6	7	8	9	Out
230	429	352	468	321	325	144	128	426	2823
Par 3	Par 4	Par 4	Par 4	Par 4	Par 4	Par 3	Par 3	Par 4	Par 33

10	11	12	13	14	15	16	17	18	In
180	336	393	418	436	105	200	385	279	2732
Par 3	Par 4	Par 4	Par 4	Par 4	Par 3	Par 3	Par 4	Par 4	Par 33

HOW TO GET THERE

nter Kingussie from north.
urn right at Duke of
Gordon Hotel and continue
o end of road.

Kingussie
Golf Club

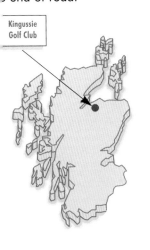

Nairn Dunbar

*I*t is perhaps of little consequence to advise that, at Nairn Dunbar, accuracy is paramount. Golfers, whatever their self-restraint, will always be tempted to snatch a few more yards off the tee, if they think they can. But they will, if they are at all sensible, only make that mistake once here!

Nairn Dunbar is a course whose fairways are flanked by gorse, scrub trees and rough. Ladies do well, not only because there is never any carry from the tee to fairway but, in adversity, they tend to knock it safely up the middle.

The course, which has three new holes taking away some of the raised sections of the old, presents a great variation on a relatively flat linksland. With a sandy subsoil and excellent greens, it offers a savoury taste of this type of Scottish golf.

On the front nine, the 4th, 5th and 6th are quite difficult with the 9th, a new Par 5 playing down to the edge of Culbin Forest Bird Reserve.

But it is the 7th that stands out on the outward half, a shortish Par 4 with a small loch on the left-hand side, its fairway lined with thick gorse. It is a slight dog-leg to a difficult green, which may require a 2-iron or even a wedge, but both would prove equally difficult to hit and hold this green.

The 10th is a 414-yard; Par 4 called Westward Ho! the most challenging on the course, also varyingly described as the 'Hole from Hell'. A carry is required to traverse a burn with OOB and gorse bushes lining the dog-legged fairway. Pot bunkers guard the green, as does the burn, which turns and runs up the left side. Replete with a comfortable new clubhouse overlooking the course, this is the place to count your good fortune in playing Nairn Dunbar – or lick your wounds.

CARD OF THE COURSE – PAR 72

1	2	3	4	5	6	7	8	9	Out
418	333	189	448	453	419	395	155	501	3311
Par 4	Par 4	Par 3	Par 4	Par 4	Par 4	Par 4	Par 3	Par 5	Par 35

10	11	12	13	14	15	16	17	18	In
414	126	381	529	346	161	503	442	499	3401
Par 4	Par 3	Par 4	Par 5	Par 4	Par 3	Par 5	Par 4	Par 5	Par 37

HOW TO GET THERE

The course lies half mile east of Nairn Town. Nairn lies on the A96 Inverness-Aberdeen major road.

Nairn Dunbar Golf Club

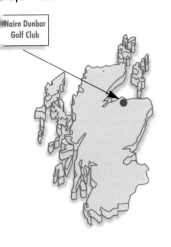

Newtonmore

*N*ewtonmore is a Highland course popular with groups and societies that travel up from the south to enjoy its flat fairways. Mainly set out on the plains of the River Spey, it makes for an easy walk. At least, that is the theory.

A flat, Highland course is not so much of a contradiction either, as Newtonmore is surrounded by glorious mountains. After the first two delightful openers, both birdie opportunities from the back tees, the course drops down dramatically to the floor of the valley. It is here you first encounter Newtonmore's premier defence, the long swathes of grass and wild flowers that border many holes. So scientifically significant is this rough that they have become sites of special interest to botanists and are protected as such. Here, whilst

searching for your ball, you will come across several species of small, rare, wild orchid. There are also wild pansies and acres of buttercups, lovely to look at but you should dread sending a ball anywhere near, as it too will become rare.

Although flat, these Speyside holes can cause a lot of problems particularly with a wind blowing up the valley. There are many substantial stands of trees dividing the fairways that can present difficulties but it is always the rough that will cost strokes.

In splendid condition, Newtonmore's fairways and greens will succumb to the straight and steady player as length is not often a prerequisite. There is said to be a high percentage of left-handed golfers at Newtonmore Golf Club who play the game of shinty in these parts.

HOW TO GET THERE

:outh: From Perth turn off A9 road
mile north of Newtonmore.

Jorth: from Inverness turn
ff at Kingussie junction and take
he A86 3 miles to Newtonmore.
;olf course is in the centre
f Newtonmore Village.

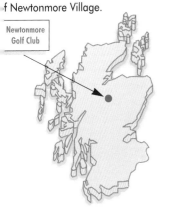

Newtonmore
Golf Club

COURSE INFORMATION & FACILITIES

Newtonmore Golf Club
Golf Course Road, Newtonmore
Highland PH20 1AT

Secretary: Richard J. Cheyne.
Tel: 01540 673878. Fax: 01540 673878.

Golf Professional Tel: 01540 673611.

Green Fees:
Weekdays – £12. Weekends – £14.
Weekdays (day) – £15. Weekends (day) – £20.

CARD OF THE COURSE – PAR 70

1	2	3	4	5	6	7	8	9	Out
252	373	409	303	373	332	403	163	365	2973
Par 4	Par 4	Par 4	Par 4	Par 4	Par 4	Par 4	Par 3	Par 4	Par 35

10	11	12	13	14	15	16	17	18	In
518	254	417	392	406	155	389	194	331	3056
Par 5	Par 4	Par 4	Par 4	Par 4	Par 3	Par 4	Par 3	Par 4	Par 35

Royal Dornoch

Golf was played at Dornoch at least as far back as 1616 when the Earl of Sutherland ordered 'cleaks and balls' to take up the game that was becoming so popular further south. This makes Royal Dornoch the third oldest golfing community in Scotland.

It was also the home course of Donald Ross, the famous golf architect who created some of North America's finest tracts such as Pinehurst No 2.

The layout of Royal Dornoch is classic links with the first eight holes following the natural grades of the old dune embankments while the remainder skirts the sandy beaches of Dornoch Bay. Plateau greens are characteristic as well as raised tees and on the Par 3's, these saucer-shaped targets prove daunting.

The 6th has to be one of the toughest tests at 165 yards with no favours for those that go left into the gorse or right down a steep bank from where double-bogies are routine.

Although the front nine is delightful, it is the back stretch where the real tests lie. Harry Vardon reckoned the 14th was 'the most natural hole in golf'. With no bunkers, there is a succession of hillocks running up to the green on the right.

The closing four holes climb over the barely covered bones of the links, and the thin turf can throw a ball in any direction no matter how well it is struck.

Tom Watson probably best summed up Royal Dornoch when he said, 'This is the most fun I have had playing golf in my whole life.'

COURSE INFORMATION & FACILITIES

Royal Dornoch Golf Club
Golf Road
Dornoch IV25 3LW.

Secretary: John S. Duncan.
Tel: 01862 810219. Fax: 01862 810792.

Golf Professional:
Tel: 01862 810902. Fax: 01862 811095.

Green Fees:
Weekdays – £40. Weekends – £50.
Handicap certificates required.

CARD OF THE COURSE – PAR 70

1	2	3	4	5	6	7	8	9	Out
331	177	414	427	354	163	463	396	496	3221
Par 4	Par 3	Par 4	Par 4	Par 4	Par 3	Par 4	Par 4	Par 5	Par 35

10	11	12	13	14	15	16	17	18	In
147	446	507	166	445	319	402	405	456	3293
Par 3	Par 4	Par 5	Par 3	Par 4	Par 4	Par 4	Par 4	Par 4	Par 35

HOW TO GET THERE

5 miles north of Inverness
ff A9. 1-2 miles after
Dornoch Firth Bridge.
Turn right off town square
hen after 100 yards turn
eft to Clubhouse.

Royal Dornoch
Golf Club

Dornoch Castle Hotel

♛♛ COMMENDED	Castle Street, Dornoch, Sutherland IV25 3SD Tel: 01862 810216 Fax: 01862 810981 *Contact: Michael Ketchin*	17 BEDROOMS

This unique hotel is situated in the main square opposite the 13th century Dornoch
Cathedral and is five minutes walk from Royal Dornoch Championship Course, and one
hour's drive from Inverness. It has one of the best restaurants in the area and an
outstanding wine list. Venison, salmon and lobster (when in season) are regular features
on the menu. All 17 bedrooms are tastefully furnished, with television, direct-dial
telephone and tea/coffee making facilities. From the panelled bar guests can watch the
regular Saturday night performance of the Dornoch Pipe Band in the summer. The
elegant lounge and sunny terrace overlook the well-kept formal garden and Dornoch
Firth. The bar and restaurant are open to non-residents. A table reservation for dinner
is advisable. Golf breaks on Royal Dornoch and other local courses available Spring and
Autumn. B&B from £35 per person.

Strathpeffer

T he village of Strathpeffer is a few miles due east of Dingwall, a popular spa town of the 1800's and still a quiet resort with plenty of comfortable hotels. It is the kind of place that attracts coach parties and elderly tourers but don't let them near the golf course.

High above the town, the car-park and clubhouse look over the valley below. There is a standing joke about parties that arrive seeking a day ticket. The starter keeps them right and sells a round.

Strathpeffer, you might have guessed, is hilly. From the 1st tee it is downhill all the way before zig-zagging back up and down the hill. Looking down on to the 1st green, there is a burn at 150 yards and

trees tight on the right but apart from that the views are lovely.

Back up the hill, the 9th, a Par 4 of 430 yards, shows a lot of rough on both sides and through the summer months the fairway is further narrowed by ticklish semi-rough.

There are a couple of blind holes on the back nine, most notably the 15th, 'The Ord' a big 421 yarder with a marker on the top of hill that should be reached. This isn't always the case so it's blind into the serious marsh on the right hand side and gorse on the left.

The 18th is a hard green to putt on, sloping right to left but it is the views all the way to the Cromarty Firth and Dingwall that really conclude this round.

HOW TO GET THERE

:0 minutes north of
nverness on the A9.
5 miles west of Dingwall,
¼ mile north of village
quare (signposted).

Strathpeffer
Golf Club

COURSE INFORMATION & FACILITIES

Strathpeffer Spa Golf Club
Strathpeffer, Ross-Shire
Scotland IV14 9AS

Secretary: Mr. Norman Roxburgh.
Tel: 01997 421396. Fax: 01997 421011.

Green Fees:
Weekdays – £12. Weekends – £12.
Weekdays (day) – £16. Weekends (day) – £16.
Some time restrictions.

CARD OF THE COURSE – PAR 65

1	2	3	4	5	6	7	8	9	Out
297	257	199	211	120	183	287	316	430	2300
Par 4	Par 4	Par 3	Par 3	Par 3	Par 3	Par 4	Par 4	Par 4	Par 32

10	11	12	13	14	15	16	17	18	In
160	231	279	306	151	419	369	271	306	2492
Par 3	Par 3	Par 4	Par 4	Par 3	Par 4	Par 4	Par 4	Par 4	Par 33

Tain

*T*ain Golf Club plays over a parcel of land on the east side of town where the alluvial deposits of the River Aldie merge with the sands of the Dornoch Firth.

This is the longest course in Ross-shire yet you are advised to hold back the driver and save yourself torn clothes and hands searching for golf balls in the whins.

The best holes on the front nine are the 2nd 3rd and 4th.

The Aldie Burns runs through the 2nd which stands at 391 yards off the medal tees but it is a very deceiving layout with a large ridge running through it then a drop of 20 foot approaching the river. This leaves another 70 yards into green.

The 3rd at 435 yards is the hardest hole on the course; a dog-leg left which is reachable in two but far safer to take three. Gorse lines the left-hand side with OOB on the right. The 4th has gorse all the way up both sides, and although the fairway is generous, this 499 yarder is a daunting task. Keep the ball on the fairway.

At the 11th we meet the Alps, a Par 4 of only 380 yards with a hidden green behind two 30-foot mountains. The green stands about 30 yards behind these.

The tidiest hole is perhaps the 16th where the burn bends around this Par 3 target.

Whisky connoisseurs will be happy to stop at Tain, home of famous Glenmorangie malt.

COURSE INFORMATION & FACILITIES

Tain Golf Club
Chapel Road, Tain
Ross-shire IV19 1PA.

Secretary:
Kathleen D. Ross.
Tel: 01862 892314.

Green Fees:
Weekdays – £20. Weekends – £24.
Weekdays (day) – £26. Weekends (day) – £30.

CARD OF THE COURSE – PAR 70

1	2	3	4	5	6	7	8	9	Out
369	391	435	499	181	309	377	189	355	3105
Par 4	Par 4	Par 4	Par 5	Par 3	Par 4	Par 4	Par 3	Par 4	Par 35

10	11	12	13	14	15	16	17	18	In
390	380	378	501	438	346	147	215	371	3166
Par 4	Par 4	Par 4	Par 5	Par 4	Par 4	Par 3	Par 3	Par 4	Par 35

HOW TO GET THERE

From South: 35 miles north of Inverness, take first right on by-pass, follow road to town centre, turn right onto Castle Brae (just past Gow's Bakery).

From North: 9 miles south of Dornoch, take first left on by-pass, follow road into town centre, turn left onto Castle Brae (just before Gow's Bakery). Once at Castle Brae course is well signposted.

Tain Golf Club

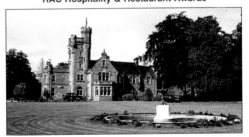

Glasgow & South West

While most visiting golfers make a bee-line for Ayrshire's flourishing golf coast, it might enlighten then to know that the Greater Glasgow and Clyde Valley area has over 80 parkland, moorland and heathland courses waiting to welcome them. From championship venues to testing 9-hole challenges, there is golf for every level of player. Combined with the abundant cultural attractions in and around the city, Glasgow presents an ideal base for a complete golfing holiday. The city is not without its golfing history and Glasgow Green was an early location for former golfers to hone their skills with 'niblick and mashie'. Now the game has spread throughout and around the city. Haggs Castle on Glasgow's south side, was the venue for the Glasgow Classic, later to become known as the Bell's Scottish Open. More recently, a new prestigious event has emerged on the banks of one of Scotland's most celebrated beauty spots. The Loch Lomond World Invitational attracts golf's greatest players to a course that, in its few short years of existence, has become known the world over for its quality and visual splendour. There are numerous other venues within a short drive of Glasgow, some of which are mentioned in the following pages, but suffice to say, a golfer would not be disappointed to bring their clubs to Glasgow. Off the fairways, the city has over 30 galleries and museums most of which are free as well as some of the friendliest pubs and clubs. There are theatres, festivals and numerous local events that are certain to make a visit most memorable. Further out from the city are the courses that surround the River Clyde such as Helensburgh, Gourock and across the water to Bute. Rothesay Golf Club on Bute has exceptional views of the surrounding hills and the Clyde Estuary. Travelling south, most serious golfers will make their way to Machrihannish on the Kintyre peninsula at least once in their lives although when they stand on the 1st tee they might wonder why! Nearby, Arran has many enjoyable venues for holiday golfers augmenting their *encounter of this idyllic island. For a shorter crossing to another Clyde Estuary island, try Great Cumbria, just off the coast near Larks where there is a lovely little 18-hole course.*

GLASGOW GAILES
HAGGS CASTLE
HILTON PARK
IRVINE
LAMLASH
LANARK
MACRIHANNISH

NEWTON STEWART
PORTPATRICK
POWFOOT
SOUTHERNESS
STRANRAER
THORNHILL
WESTERN GAILES

Glasgow Gailes

*I*t might seem confusing that a club called Glasgow Gailes is more than 30 miles from the city. The explanation is that the original Glasgow Golf Club, in 1892, decided to open a second facility for its members on the Ayrshire coast. The public course that they had been playing over in Alexandra Park in Glasgow had become a little too popular, hence the move.

The now exclusive Glasgow Golf Club also plays at Killermont in Bearsden in Glasgow, a course without provision for visitors. But its sister club on the Ayrshire coast makes guests most welcome.

Laid out on the coast, just south of the town of Irvine, Glasgow Gailes has the added benefit of remaining free of frost throughout the year due to the temperate effects of the Gulf Stream.

The course is lined with heather and gorse, which form the major fairway hazards. But it is the luxurious greens, beautiful to behold amidst the hoary growth, that provide much of the action and adversity on this course. Apart from the 7th and 10th which are almost identical, no two holes are the same at Gailes. Each hole presents something singular in its design and challenge. The 14th is a worthy Par 5 of 526 yards off the Medal tees. Two humps stand sentinel 70 yards short of the green, which can be reached with two good shots onto the large putting area.

With recent improvements to the clubhouse, Glasgow Gailes is as good as any of the courses to be found on this wonderful stretch of coast and should be included on an Ayrshire itinerary.

COURSE INFORMATION & FACILITIES

Glasgow Golf Club
Gailes, Irvine
Ayrshire KA11 5AE

Secretary: D.W. Deas.
Tel: 0141 942 2011. Fax: 0141 942 0770.

Golf Professional Tel: 01294 311561.

Green Fees: ·
Weekdays – £40. Weekends (afternoons only) – £45.
Weekdays (day) – £50.

CARD OF THE COURSE – PAR 71

1	2	3	4	5	6	7	8	9	Out
345	349	425	414	530	152	403	343	304	3265
Par 4	Par 4	Par 4	Par 4	Par 5	Par 3	Par 4	Par 4	Par 4	Par 36

10	11	12	13	14	15	16	17	18	In
422	419	179	334	526	152	413	365	435	3245
Par 4	Par 4	Par 3	Par 4	Par 5	Par 3	Par 4	Par 4	Par 4	Par 35

HOW TO GET THERE

A77 from Glasgow to Kilmarnock.
A71 to Irvine.
A78 towards Ayr and leave at the first exit.
Take Marine Drive. Glasgow Gailes is off
Marine Drive to the right.

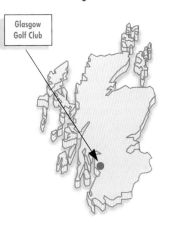

Glasgow
Golf Club

Haggs Castle

*I*t is no small accolade for Haggs Castle Golf Club that it has hosted several events on the European Tour, back in the 1980's including the Bell's Scottish Open in 1986.

Situated on the south side of Glasgow and very accessible for the motorway system, it is one of the best inland courses available so near to the city.

Its holes are carved from very pleasant parkland with a variety of dog-legs both right and left through tree-lined fairways. Another challenging feature is its small greens that are fairly well bunkered.

The 10th, 11th, and 14th are excellent holes that appeal for the demand off the tee. With out of bounds very much a factor on the 10th and 11th great care is required with the drive. The 14th is a dog-leg left through an avenue of trees and into the wind, this can require a three iron or wood.

The closing stretch is slightly kinder with the 18th, one of the easier Par 5's on the course reachable in two for the better player.

For those with interest in some of Glasgow's many cultural features, the club is also very well placed. The baronial Haggs Castle is a free museum located nearby. Built in 1585, it is a period museum for children, centering on educational activities. Nearby also is the much-praised Museum of Education at Scotland Street School. Continuing along the A77 is Pollock Country Park in which is contained the famous Burrell Collection.

COURSE INFORMATION & FACILITIES

Haggs Castle Golf Club
70 Dumbreck Road
Glasgow G41 4SN.

Secretary: Ian Harvey.
Tel: 0141 427 1157. Fax: 0141 427 1157.

Golf Professional Tel: 0141 427 3355.

Green Fees:
Weekdays – £27.
Weekdays (Day) – £38.

CARD OF THE COURSE – PAR 72

1	2	3	4	5	6	7	8	9	Out
483	169	363	476	409	431	159	431	341	3262
Par 5	Par 3	Par 4	Par 5	Par 4	Par 4	Par 3	Par 4	Par 4	Par 36

10	11	12	13	14	15	16	17	18	In
383	372	172	323	425	340	363	348	476	3202
Par 4	Par 4	Par 3	Par 4	Par 4	Par 4	Par 4	Par 4	Par 5	Par 36

HOW TO GET THERE

A8, M77 Junction 1 – end of road turn left and then immediately right.

Haggs Castle
Golf Club

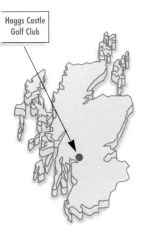

Hilton Park

When the members of Hilton Park Golf Club first began to travel out to their new courses, built in 1927 to accommodate golfers whose playing fields had been warranted for the building of a new Glasgow housing estate, they must have thought they had passed away and gone in the best possible direction.

The club is situated on the road to the Trossachs and Loch Lomond yet only a few miles north of the bustling city. This is the beauty of Scotland, where you can relish such scenery in less than half an hour's drive from busy Clydebank or Sauchiehall Street

The main course here, the Hilton, sits on a knoll 500 feet above sea level and many of the holes overlook the Clyde Valley with Glasgow's skyline to the south, the Kilpatrick Hills to the west and the Campsies to the east. To the North is the noble summit of Ben Lomond with the Trossachs nearby. With such views comes the prospect of hard climbing but it does not seem to discourage the happy souls who play here. The crest of the course is reminiscent of a balding head lined with thin strips of thatch. This is the main hazard atop, bands of small trees, pine and birch, delineating the fairways.

James Braid was responsible for the design, in fact of 27 of the 36 holes available here, including the shorter but testing Allander course, Par 69, SSS 66. The Par 3 6th on the Hilton is probably his finest touch with 220 yards to cover through the Khyber Pass, as it is called. The 13th is also a cracker with 415 yards off the medal tees but on a typical, windy day at this elevation, the longest hitters have trouble.

COURSE INFORMATION & FACILITIES

Hilton Park Golf Club
Stockiemuir Road, Milngavie
Glasgow G62 7HB.

Secretary:
Mrs. J. A. Warnock.
Tel: 0141 956 4657.

Golf Professional Tel: 0141 956 5125.

Green Fees:
Weekdays – £20. Weekdays (Day) – £28.
Society Rates: £20 per round, £28 per day.

CARD OF THE COURSE – PAR 70

1	2	3	4	5	6	7	8	9	Out
496	386	403	177	422	220	306	307	314	3031
Par 5	Par 4	Par 4	Par 3	Par 4	Par 3	Par 4	Par 4	Par 4	Par 35

10	11	12	13	14	15	16	17	18	In
340	373	157	415	329	363	498	184	364	3023
Par 4	Par 4	Par 3	Par 4	Par 4	Par 4	Par 5	Par 3	Par 4	Par 35

HOW TO GET THERE

A809 approximately 8 miles north west of Glasgow.

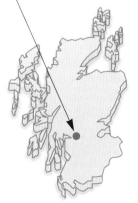

Hilton Park Golf Club

Irvine

*I*rvine 'Bogside' Golf Club nestles near some of the big names in Ayrshire with Royal Troon and Old Prestwick being 'just doon the road'. There is no doubt that this stretch of Scottish coastline was ideal for the game of golf and the locals have made excellent use of the linksland.

One of the additional bonuses for the area is that most courses play all year round with the benign waters of the Gulf Stream keeping the greens frost-free.

Built between the town, a racecourse and the muddy River Irvine, Bogside's situation isn't quite perfect but when you behold the sensual terrain that this course plays over, you then notice little else.

The 6th is a remarkable Par 4 that flies over the crest of a hill before dropping 40 ft from the promontory on to the fairway. Club players lay up and then take a long iron onto the green. At 411 yards, it's not a monster but each stoke needs to be precisely and fearlessly struck.

The ground rolls and bobs over ancient dune terrain, divided by gorse and lots of heather. Every hole is an individual. Even in the heart of winter the greens are reasonable but, during the season, they are sensational.

If it's a calm day you can score well but perched as it is on a wide, open rise with wind caressing every corner, its Par 71 offers an SSS of 73.

om **Kilmarnock:** A71 to Warrix interchange
ıst roundabout). Take 3rd turning onto A78. After approx.
miles take Eglinton exit. Take 1st left and continue to next
undabout. Take 2nd turning into Irvine. Continue into
vine for approx 1 mile. Turn right into Sandy Road,
·oceed for approx. 200 yards. At bend turn left onto
ıclassified road. Club is along this road on right.
om **Barrhead/Irvine Road:** Continue on A736 until
·riving at Sourlie roundabout. Take 2nd turning and
·oceed to next roundabout. Take 4th turning
to Long Drive. Proceed for approx. 2 miles
next roundabout (Eglinton interchange),
en as above.
om **Greenock/Irvine**
ɔad or Ayr/Irvine
ɔad: Continue
ı A78 to Irvine/
lwinning
⟨it at
glington
terchange,
en as above.

Irvine
Golf Club

COURSE INFORMATION & FACILITIES

The Irvine Golf Club
Bogside
North Ayrshire KA12 85N

Secretary: Andrew Morton.
Tel: 01294 275979.

Golf Professional Tel: 01294 275626.

Green Fees:
Weekdays – £30. Weekends – £45.
Weekdays (day) – £45.

CARD OF THE COURSE – PAR 71

1	2	3	4	5	6	7	8	9	Out
418	476	358	289	279	411	322	165	456	3174
Par 4	Par 5	Par 4	Par 4	Par 4	Par 4	Par 4	Par 3	Par 4	Par 36

10	11	12	13	14	15	16	17	18	In
373	465	368	429	382	337	156	391	333	3234
Par 4	Par 4	Par 4	Par 4	Par 4	Par 4	Par 3	Par 4	Par 4	Par 35

Lamlash

As a golfing escape, Arran is one of the best and few people have, as yet, discovered it. The island's ability to offer several 'fun' golf courses surrounded by spectacular scenery and with an ambience of peace and tranquillity is its lasting appeal.

Seven courses are evenly distributed making it possible to experience the island as well as appreciate its golf facilities. Each of the courses offers pleasant, holiday golf where you can work on your game and relax at the same time.

South of Brodick is the hamlet of Lamlash. The course is visible from the road and it is worth slowing down to savour the splendid views across Lamlash Golf Course to the Holy Island, sitting in the Clyde Estuary beyond. Of any of Scotland's golf views, this must be one of the best.

Looking at the scorecard, it might appear short but there are many testing holes here, particularly the long Par 3's.

The 1st is a good opener best played as a slight dog-leg right although it looks straight from tee to green. It's a par 4 with a long second shot so it plays its full length.

The 5th, with its tee sited beside the road, lets you see all of the green, which is in a hollow with rough and a burn to carry so it needs just the right shot.

The best hole of the back nine is perhaps the 16th, a Par 3 of only 97 yards, so simple that it can become difficult.

COURSE INFORMATION & FACILITIES

Lamlash Golf Club
Ilse of Arran
KA27 8JU.

Secretary: J. Henderson.
Tel: 01770 600272. Fax: 01770 600196.

Golf Professional Tel: 0000 000000.

Green Fees:
Weekdays – £10. Weekends – £12.
Weekdays (day) – £14. Weekends (day) – £18.

CARD OF THE COURSE – PAR 64

1	2	3	4	5	6	7	8	9	Out
346	189	389	183	208	325	294	266	355	2555
Par 4	Par 3	Par 4	Par 3	Par 3	Par 4	Par 4	Par 4	Par 4	Par 33

10	11	12	13	14	15	16	17	18	In
276	271	233	191	215	275	102	226	296	2086
Par 4	Par 4	Par 3	Par 3	Par 3	Par 4	Par 3	Par 3	Par 4	Par 31

HOW TO GET THERE

miles south of Ferry
erminal at Brodick,
sle of Arran. Located
n the River Clyde.
Departure point Ardrossan.

Lamlash
Golf Club

GLENISLE HOTEL
Lamlash, Isle of Arran KA27 8LS
Telephone: (01770) 600559

A warm Scottish welcome awaits you at The Glenisle Hotel.
The large attractive garden overlooks Lamlash Bay and Holy Isle.
Our restaurant offers superb cuisine with a wide range of dishes
to suit all tastes.
Our cosy cocktail bar with log fire is the ideal place to relax
with a favourite drink or to enjoy an aperitif before dinner.
All bedrooms are attractively furnished with private facilities,
colour TV, radio and tea/coffee makers – many enjoy magnificent
sea views towards Holy Isle.

Lanark

*L*anark's course has a far-flung reputation spread mainly by word of mouth and good golfers from around the world make their way here, especially when an Open Championship is held in nearby Ayrshire.

Over the past twenty years a regular Open qualifying course, Lanark offers many of the conditions found on a links course with sandy subsoil and a healthy moorland loam. The 'Moor' as it was referred to, was cattle grazing land and this, no doubt, has contributed to the vigorous tone of the turf.

The course went through various evolutions until 1897 when Old Tom Morris was hired for three days to upgrade it to an 18-hole tract. He was paid the grand sum of £3/10 shillings for the work, a munificent sum as his usual rate was only £1.00 a day.

Ben Sayers later made his contribution and, in the 1920's, James Braid added length and bunkers.

Tinto is the name of the 8th, a 530-yard Par 5 that offers little resistance to well-placed balls unlike some of the more deceptive Par 4's.

The 10th is a 152-yard, Par 3 looking through a channel of trees to an elevated green which is set off by three large bunkers. Tintock Tap is the mountain seen away in the distance. The 18th, at 216 yards is an unusual Par 3 finish with a plaza of a green directly beneath the clubhouse window with its attentive onlookers. Wave if you make par.

COURSE INFORMATION & FACILITIES

Lanark Golf Club
The Moor, Whitelees Road
Lanark ML11 7RX.

Secretary: George Cuthill.
Tel: 01555 663219. Fax: 01555 663219.

Golf Professional:
Tel: 01555 661456. Fax: 01555 661456.

Green Fees:
Weekdays – £24. Weekdays (Day) – £36.
No weekend visitors.

CARD OF THE COURSE – PAR 70

1	2	3	4	5	6	7	8	9	Out
360	467	409	457	318	377	141	530	360	3419
Par 4	Par 4	Par 4	Par 4	Par 4	Par 4	Par 3	Par 5	Par 4	Par 36

10	11	12	13	14	15	16	17	18	In
152	397	362	362	399	470	337	309	216	3004
Par 3	Par 4	Par 4	Par 4	Par 4	Par 4	Par 4	Par 4	Par 3	Par 34

HOW TO GET THERE

From M74 take the A73, follow signs for Lanark. Follow signs for town centre, turn right before Somerfield store onto Whitelees Road (3/4 mile to course). From M8 take the A73 at Newhouse, follow signs for Lanark. Stay on A73 and turn left just past Somerfield store onto Whitelees Road.

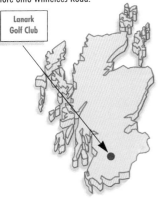

Machrihanish

To stand on the 1st tee at Machrihanish with the Atlantic breakers pounding on your left, a long beach carry dead-ahead and an ever-present wind ready to whip a high strike across the fairway and into the rough, there is little wonder that this is most often regarded as Scotland's premier opening hole.

J. H. Taylor had much to do with this coastal layout but it was Old Tom Morris who was first contracted in 1879 and on seeing the wide expanse of links, declared that the area was "specially designed by the Almighty for playing golf". Even now, beholding the course, you would still share Old Tom's sentiments.

It is amongst the dunes that players begin to take pleasure in this marvellous course. The 3rd terminates just before the beach often with threatening cumulous gathering out at sea. The 4th, a delightful Par 3 is an island of green amongst a sea of long, tangled grass.

Blind shots are prevalent throughout Machrihanish and can make for first round frustration but all the more reason to plan two or three rounds here. Having said that, the course changes with every breath of wind but there are few finer courses with which to become aquainted with.

In case the driving distance from Edinburgh or Glasgow to the Mull of Kintyre puts you off, be aware that there is a daily flight, from Glasgow Airport direct to Machrihanish.

COURSE INFORMATION & FACILITIES

The Machrihanish Golf Club
Machrihanish, Campbeltown
Argyll PA28 6PT

Secretary: Anna Anderson.
Tel: 01586 810213. Fax: 01586-810221.
(for bookings)

Golf Professional Tel: 01586-810277.

Green Fees: Weekdays – £21. Saturday – £36.
Weekdays (day) – £30. Saturday (day) – £36.

CARD OF THE COURSE – PAR 70

1	2	3	4	5	6	7	8	9	Out
423	395	376	123	385	315	432	337	354	3140
Par 4	Par 4	Par 4	Par 3	Par 4	Par 4	Par 4	Par 4	Par 4	Par 35

10	11	12	13	14	15	16	17	18	In
497	197	505	370	442	167	233	362	315	3088
Par 5	Par 3	Par 5	Par 4	Par 4	Par 3	Par 3	Par 4	Par 4	Par 35

HOW TO GET THERE

Approximately three hours drive from Glasgow. The most direct route is by the A82 to Tarbet on Loch Lomond, then the A83 via Inveraray and Lochgilphead.

Machrihanish
Golf Club

Newton Stewart

Although this seems an easy enough course that is ideal for holiday golf outing, Newton Stewart comes with its own set of idiosyncrasies that any golfer will enjoy.

Laid out around a hilly area, it is a pleasant piece of rustic parkland with very little earnest climbing. Apart from the hike from the 2nd green to the 3rd tee there is only a modest elevation all the way up to the 10th.

The course is set up for golfers to enjoy themselves and not get hung-up in rough although there are patches of gorse that will catch really wild shots.

The 1st and 2nd fairways are edged with OOB while holes such as the 4th and 5th can be approached on either fairway. The 7th has OOB on the left but there is plenty of room for manoeuvre along this stretch.

The course's apex comes at the turn. Around this corner, the 9th plays up the side of a pond, a Par 4 of 360 yards with a stream running diagonally across the fairway. The green is off-set and there is a choice of playing across the dyke or taking the easy route. The Par 3, 10th, called the Gushet is one of the original holes playing over a burn with the pond on the left.

The town of Newton Stewart sits on the banks of the River. Game fishing is popular in this area. The best access point into Galloway Forest Park, famous for hills, lochs, moorland and forest that are a haven for wildlife, is via the A714 north of Newton Stewart to Glen Trool village then on to Glen Trool Lodge.

COURSE INFORMATION & FACILITIES

Newton Stewart Golf Club
Kirroughtree Avenue, Newton Stewart
Dumfries & Galloway D68 6PF.

Secretary: J. Tait. Tel: 01671 403376.
Clubhouse Tel: 01671 402172.

Green Fees:
Weekdays – £17. Weekends – £20.
Weekdays (day) – £20. Weekends (day) – £24.
Society Rates: On Request.

CARD OF THE COURSE – PAR 69

1	2	3	4	5	6	7	8	9	Out
346	360	177	371	426	175	353	383	337	2928
Par 4	Par 4	Par 3	Par 4	Par 4	Par 3	Par 4	Par 4	Par 4	Par 34

10	11	12	13	14	15	16	17	18	In
152	520	197	523	405	328	345	164	325	2959
Par 3	Par 5	Par 3	Par 5	Par 4	Par 4	Par 4	Par 3	Par 4	Par 35

HOW TO GET THERE

Newton Stewart is on the A75 Euroroute Carlisle to Stranraer. The course itself is very easily reached from the A75.

Newton Stewart
Golf Club

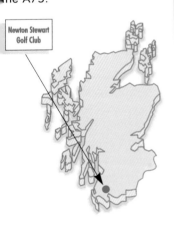

Portpatrick

The village of Portpartick is a quintessential holiday retreat with enchanting lanes and cottages built around a tranquil little harbour.

The course sits above the town on a headland with steep cliffs marking its western perimeter. Perched out in the Irish Sea on a long, rocky-shored annex of land known as the Rhinns of Galloway, Portpatrick (Dunskey) Golf Club catches the best of the Gulf Stream's warmth; and its wind. It presents a variety of terrain, caught between rolling moorland and seaside heath. The rough is a devastating combination of lush green grass and gorse and it has an ally in the near-ever-present gusts, which aid in the regular abduction of golf balls.

Dunskey is known for its tricky par 3's.

The 7th is a good short hole at 165 yards with a ledge to the left that may gather some errant shots but it is ultimately safer to stray right if anywhere.

The 15th is of only 100 yards but it can be the toughest hole on the course with little room for error on a hidden and wind-dried green. The 13th is a place to catch your breath before it gets taken away again – by the fantastic views from this hole. The panorama of the green sitting above Sandeel Bay makes the pulse quicken as will the hike up to the 14th.

Dunskey is not a long course but that does not mean a lot in such a wind-buffeted corner of Scotland. Pro-ams are regularly staged over its curvaceous tracts but they have never managed to beat the 64-course record.

COURSE INFORMATION & FACILITIES

Portpatrick (Dunskey) Golf Club
Portpatrick
Wigtownshire DG9 8TB.

Secretary: Mr. J. A. Horberry.
Tel: 01776 810273. Fax: 01776 810811.

Green Fees:
Weekdays – £17. Weekends – £20.
Weekdays (day) – £25. Weekends (day) – £30.
Handicap Certificate required.
Some time restrictions.

CARD OF THE COURSE – PAR 70

1	2	3	4	5	6	7	8	9	Out
393	375	544	160	405	382	165	377	311	3112
Par 4	Par 4	Par 5	Par 3	Par 4	Par 4	Par 3	Par 4	Par 4	Par 35

10	11	12	13	14	15	16	17	18	In
329	163	390	293	293	101	393	301	535	2798
Par 4	Par 3	Par 4	Par 4	Par 4	Par 3	Par 4	Par 4	Par 5	Par 35

HOW TO GET THERE

From South: M6 - A75 to Stranraer/Portpatrick, signposted after Glenluce By-Pass. On entering the village fork right at War Memorial and look for signpost.
From North: A77 to Stranraer and Portpatrick. Then as above.

Portpatrick Golf Club

***

Fernhill Hotel

PORTPATRICK, WIGTOWNSHIRE

Only a stroll from the clifftop Portpatrick *(Dunskey)* Golf course **FERNHILL** is the ideal base for all your golfing holiday desires. Concessions available at five local clubs and inclusive weekend, midweek and very special weekly breaks available.

Superb conservatory restaurant serving fresh local produce and fine wines, well appointed comfortable rooms and friendly welcoming staff.

FERNHILL HOTEL · PORTPATRICK
WIGTOWNSHIRE DG9 8TB
TEL: (+44) 01776 810220
FAX: (+44) 01776 810596

Scotland's Commended Taste of Scotland

INVESTORS IN PEOPLE

Powfoot

Wandering your way from the town of Annan through the village of Cummertrees you overlook the terminal end of the Solway Firth, you have arrived at Powfoot Golf Club.

This is a prominent links course in the southwest, distinguished as a championship venue which plays through a veritable sea of gorse.

There are actually only 14 holes that are true links while the back four holes are more parkland in nature. As with most Braid designs, the start is temperate, a hole to iron out the snatches and cracks.

You will need poise for hole 2, a 477 yard Par 5 which faces south overlooking the water. It is tight after the tee shot but, unless the wind is blasting out of the west, a steady blow should see you onto the green.

The 3rd plays along the shore in a west to east direction as does the 4th then it is into the thick of this compact layout with nothing but blooming gorse to be seen.

As with many links courses, it is not possible to view some bunkers from the tee so it is expedient to study a course plan. The 7th green approach is thick with them, eight in all, making this pure target golf on a Par 3 as the top of the flag is all that is usually visible.

This part of the southwest enjoys its own weather and is sometimes referred to as the Costa del Solway. While other courses are wondering why they put in sprinkler systems, Powfoot can be as dry as dust, making it more difficult to judge the run of a ball. Catering at Powfoot is of the homemade variety, usually offering some traditional Scottish cuisine and the homemade lentil soup is worth investigating.

HOW TO GET THERE

...low M6 north from Carlisle until A75
...n turn off for Stranraer/Dumfries.
...low road to Annan/Dumfries until 2nd
...n off for Annan, continue and take first
...ht to Cummertrees and Powfoot on
...24. After approx. 3 miles ignore first
...n for Powfoot, continue until passing
...der railway bridge then turn
...rp left on road leading to
...lf Course.

Powfoot
Golf Club

COURSE INFORMATION & FACILITIES

Powfoot Golf Club
Annan
Dumfriesshire DG12 5QE

Manager:
Tel: 01461 700276. Fax: 01461 700276.

Golf Professional Tel: 01461 700327.

Green Fees: Weekdays – £20. Weekends – £20.
Weekdays (day) – £27. Weekly Ticket £80.
Some time restrictions.

CARD OF THE COURSE – PAR 71

1	2	3	4	5	6	7	8	9	Out
349	477	442	357	272	349	154	360	402	3162
Par 4	Par 5	Par 4	Par 4	Par 4	Par 4	Par 3	Par 4	Par 4	Par 36

10	11	12	13	14	15	16	17	18	In
428	313	156	339	501	200	429	335	403	3104
Par 4	Par 4	Par 3	Par 4	Par 5	Par 3	Par 4	Par 4	Par 4	Par 35

Southerness

Southerness was always considered one of the great 'hidden gems' of Scotland, a course that only the lucky or the well-informed knew about. But a reputation such as this soon creates a contradiction in terms and now keen golfers congregate from all parts of the world to play this marvellous layout.

It is still, however, out-of-the-way and generally quiet, free of crowds or tediously slow play. There are few locals, only a caravan site as a neighbour and miles and miles of unspoilt vistas over the Solway Firth.

Set on a flat piece of links land and fringed by a wonderful beach, Southerness is a combination of challenge and prospect that will cure any jaded golf palate.

The designer Mackenzie Ross, who brought Turnberry back to life after its wartime service as a potato field, built this course following the war. His remit was to create a test to meet modern conditions. Therefore, this is a long exercise with at least eight Par 4's over 400 yards. The alliance of wind, heather, marsh and distance makes it very demanding but, on a decent day, most will relish the opportunity to try and keep to the fairway.

The Par 4, 12th, with the flag flapping hard, many will rightly consider the course's zenith. It is a right-cornered dog-leg flanked by heather and grasses that plays longer than its 400 yard length. Any temptation to 'cut the corner' must be soberly considered. Marsh and heather, impossible to escape easily, will add to the price of deviation from the prescribed route.

DUMFRIES

COURSE INFORMATION & FACILITIES

Southerness Golf Club
Kirkbeah
Dumfries DG2 8AZ.

Secretary: W. D. Ramage.
Tel: 01387 880677. Fax: 01387 880644.

Green Fees:
Weekdays – £25. Weekends – £35.
Weekdays (day) – £25. Weekends (day) – £35.
Handicap certificates required.

CARD OF THE COURSE – PAR 69

1	2	3	4	5	6	7	8	9	Out
393	450	408	169	496	405	215	371	435	3342
Par 4	Par 4	Par 4	Par 3	Par 5	Par 4	Par 3	Par 4	Par 4	Par 35

10	11	12	13	14	15	16	17	18	In
168	390	421	467	458	217	433	175	495	3224
Par 3	Par 4	Par 4	Par 4	Par 4	Par 3	Par 4	Par 3	Par 5	Par 34

HOW TO GET THERE

eave A75 at Dumfries and
ollow A710 signposted
olway Coast and follow for
5 miles south. Southerness
s signposted (approx. 1 mile).

Southerness
Golf Club

Stranraer

Stranraer, like some of its near neighbours, deserves more attention than it gets but this corner of Scotland, despite such great courses, remains fairly quiet.

This is a superb championship layout with the further distinction of being the last course to be designed by James Braid before his death. In fact, he never got to see the finished result. Many players will tell you this is one of his best.

In spite of the fact that it is on the shores of a saltwater loch, Stranraer does not pertain, to being a links course.

Laid out on farmland with many stands of mature trees, it is best described as parkland with fairly undulating ground

There are four holes that are played along the loch shore; these dropping down quite dramatically from the escarpment that hold the rest of the course.

The 5th is the signature hole looking over Loch Ryan north to Ailsa Craig, the island of Arran and beyond. From an elevated tee, this Par 4 plays down to a tight fairway pinched between the loch and steep, heavily roughed banking. If you miss all this and don't get caught in the two right-side bunkers, you have hit a good tee shot.

The 15th is a Par 3, and although it is only 165 yards, accuracy is paramount. The ground slopes away steeply on both sides of the green, severely on the shore side.

From the relatively new, two story clubhouse with its panoramic lounge area, you can enjoy views of a large part of the course.

CARD OF THE COURSE – PAR 70

1	2	3	4	5	6	7	8	9	Out
319	338	420	324	397	160	381	315	458	3112
Par 4	Par 4	Par 4	Par 4	Par 4	Par 3	Par 4	Par 4	Par 4	Par 35

10	11	12	13	14	15	16	17	18	In
346	377	185	335	513	165	470	462	343	3196
Par 4	Par 4	Par 3	Par 4	Par 5	Par 3	Par 4	Par 4	Par 4	Par 35

HOW TO GET THERE

The course can be approached from Stranraer by taking the A718 road to Kirkcolm

Stranraer Golf Club

Thornhill

Thornhill is another unknown jewel, a charmer of a course for those that have discovered it, taken a shine to it, and then kept quiet.

The village of Thornhill is a staging post on the A76, Dumfries to Kilmarnock road, and not a busy route in itself. The mid-Nithsdale area is well known for fishing, sightseeing and the land farmed by Robert Burns before he moved to Dumfries.

Set above the valley, the delightful fairways and greens scan the tops of pinewoods over to the Keir Hills and Lowther Hills beyond.

It is one of the friendliest clubs to the touring golfer who has taken the time to seek it out. The little clubhouse looks more like a cricket pavilion and inside it is cosy and welcoming with a fine standard of catering in the newly refurbished dining room.

The course fairly zigzags over the hillsides, across dykes and through trees. It is a combination of parkland and moorland that can suit anybody's game, with wide fairways and manageable hazards, enjoyable for the less experienced but a good test for the proficient.

A hole to be savoured here is the Par 4, 4th at 426 yards, with OOB on both sides off the tee. The fairway narrows at the dog-leg before an open ditch then it is on to an elevated green. This two tiered platform is the best on the front nine.

On the back, you have the Par 3, 14th, at 156 yards and in a wind this can vary from an 8 to a 5-iron.

HOW TO GET THERE

12 miles north of Dumfries
on the A76 Dumfries to
Kilmarnock Road.
The course is 1 mile
from the village cross.

Thornhill
Golf Club

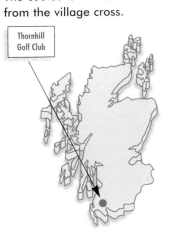

COURSE INFORMATION & FACILITIES

Thornhill Golf Club Blacknest Course
Blacknest, Thornhill
Dumfriesshire DG3 5DW

Co-Ordinator: Dave Balfour.

Green Fees:
Weekdays (day) – £20.
Weekends (day) – £24.
Some time restrictions apply.

CARD OF THE COURSE – PAR 71

1	2	3	4	5	6	7	8	9	Out
158	477	359	426	267	421	317	160	332	2917
Par 3	Par 5	Par 4	Par 4	Par 4	Par 4	Par 4	Par 3	Par 4	Par 35

10	11	12	13	14	15	16	17	18	In
396	342	363	429	156	497	191	266	528	3168
Par 4	Par 4	Par 4	Par 4	Par 3	Par 5	Par 3	Par 4	Par 5	Par 36

Western Gailes

Situated only two miles north of Royal Troon and close enough to Old Prestwick and Turnberry, it would be understandable if Western Gailes was overshadowed by these well-established international venues. But through the years, amongst golf purists, Western Gailes' reputation has ascended as one of the finest examples of a true Scottish links, and, for those in the know; a course not to be missed.

The regard for the place has perhaps grown strongest in the USA where, mainly by word of mouth and spoke of as 'a real hidden Scottish gem', each summer, there is a continuous flow of American golfers sampling this fine tract.

The view from the elevated clubhouse takes in the long strip of golf course and its grassy swells to the mountainous crests of the island of Arran. On the course, the first few holes play north with heather, gorse and wispy, ensnaring marram grass providing the hazards. Then it turns into folds of high, sandy dunes interspersed with inventive, sensuous greens that are defended by hungry little pot bunkers. Three burns and a ditch cross the course at least seven times and feature more significantly from the 8th on, adding to the fascination of this magnificently natural layout.

The course was designed by Willie Park Snr. and Jr. and remodelled only twenty-odd years ago when a new road took away part of the original layout. The Club was founded in 1897 and in 1903, Harry Vardon took the prize in the first major competition. Since then Western Gailes has hosted the Curtis Cup, PGA Championship, British Seniors, Scottish and Boys Championships and the Ladies Home International and it is a qualifying course when the Open is held at Royal Troon and Turnberry.

HOW TO GET THERE

3 miles north of Troon (A78).

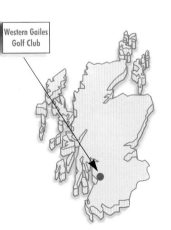

Western Gailes
Golf Club

COURSE INFORMATION & FACILITIES

Western Gailes Golf Club
Irvine
Ayrshire KA11 5AE

Secretary: Andrew M. McBean, C.A.
Tel: 01294 311649. Fax: 01294 312312.

Green Fees:
Weekdays – £50. Weekends – £60.
Weekdays (day) – £80.
Letter of introduction required. Some time restrictions.

CARD OF THE COURSE – PAR 71

1	2	3	4	5	6	7	8	9	Out
304	434	365	355	453	506	171	365	336	3289
Par 4	Par 4	Par 4	Par 4	Par 4	Par 5	Par 3	Par 4	Par 4	Par 36

10	11	12	13	14	15	16	17	18	In
348	445	436	141	562	194	404	443	377	3350
Par 4	Par 4	Par 4	Par 3	Par 5	Par 3	Par 4	Par 4	Par 4	Par 35

Index

Index

Notes